# Lest We Forget:
## A Ranger Medic's Story

# Leo "Doc" Jenkins

## Dedication

To the men of the 75th Ranger Regiment. This is for you. This is my story but it is all of our stories. My sincerest hope is that even if we have never met that you can relate to the words that follow. This was written for you, my brothers, in an effort that those outside of our fraternity may better understand our unique and valuable personalities. Thank you from the bottom of my heart for all that you have done as my mentors, as my friends, as my brothers.

"From this day to the ending of the world,
But we in it shall be remembered-
We few, we happy few, we band of brothers;
For he today that sheds his blood with me shall be my brother:"
~William Shakespeare

# Foreword

In late 2007 I attempted to work through issues that I was having related to my assimilation from the military to the college lifestyle by writing a book. This book was never finished due to my hard drive crashing. This time I have decided to compose my thoughts on a blog so that in the event that my archaic computer decides once again to commit cyber suicide, I will not be forced into another three day "coping" binder.

The transition from the military to college was a difficult era. At that particular time in my life I felt a great deal of cognitive dissonance for having left the military to join the very social environment which we spoke of with disdain in our un-air conditioned tents in Iraq. I felt like I had betrayed my brothers, abandoned them in their time of need. Telling the true stories of my experiences as a Ranger medic in Iraq and Afghanistan absolutely helped me to process and cope with what had taken place. It was also a very emotionally draining process. The feeling of writing just a couple of pages was analogous to running a marathon. This was a big reason why I decided to not rewrite that book. It has been over five years and I finally feel emotionally strong enough to rewrite some of those events. However, the purpose of this project is not dedicated to the assimilation process from special operations to the civilian world.

My hopes here are multifaceted. It is very important that the stories of the brave men with whom I served be told. The greatest disrespect that we can show our nations warriors is to forget their sacrifices. Throughout the course of these factual, real life stories, I hope to shed light on the mistakes that have been made, the lessons learned and the projection of the world through the eyes of a warrior that no longer has a war to fight. It is important to know that the men of special operations are not superhuman, unfeeling robots. They are young men with a spectacular job. A great deal is asked of them but at the end of the day they breathe the same air as everyone else. There will be foul language and obscure references. There will be stories that involve drinking, fighting, nudity, and other crimes that I was fortunate enough to not be charged with. Enjoy.

......

# Chapter 1- Cuts Marked in the March of Men

The sticky fluid I felt between my thumb and forefinger meant that I had found the vein. Blood has a much more viscous texture than sweat. With the moon providing almost zero illumination tonight, the subtle tackiness on the fingers of my ungloved hand was the only indicator that I had found my target. He didn't flinch when I perforated his left arm despite hitting him with the biggest needle in my bag, one that is typically reserved for relieving the thoracic pressure built up by a punctured lung. This thing had the girth of a McDonald's straw. Later I would explain to my superior medical officer that the near pitch-black environment was the reason why Greg received a lawn dart in his antecubital fossa but really it was because he was always a dick to me.

Less than an hour ago we were sitting packed into the fuselage of a C130 cargo plane. What a spectacular sight it must have been from the ground to see the silhouettes of hundreds of Army Rangers descending from the heavens and landing on that airfield. With very little visibility and even less control of those old parachutes, accidents in the air are bound to happen. As we plummeted to earth I found myself literally running on top of another Ranger's parachute in an event known as "sky sharking." I'm not entirely sure of the physics behind the reaction but two parachutes cannot stay inflated atop one another. I watched in helpless terror as his shoot collapsed sending him directly to the earth like a shot put. There was nothing that I could do. When I landed I quickly collected my parachute and removed my rifle from the scabbard that was affixed to my left hip during the jump. The aid bag that sat nestled at my thighs during that long flight was unhooked and on my back in a matter of seconds. As quickly as I hit the ground I was moving. I had to link up with the rest of my platoon. The airborne infiltration was just the ride to the office, now it was time to go to work.

En route to the objective rally point I found a young private kneeled over another man whose parachute was still attached to his motionless body. As I moved closer I heard the eerie sounds of the unconscious Ranger's agonal breathing pattern. His respirations were a mix of gasping and snoring. As I took a knee by his side I realized this must have been the guy that I sky sharked. Fuck. Instructing the young private who was already there to hold his head in an effort to keep his neck from moving, I began my assessment. I didn't feel any bones out of place or any bleeding. Just as fast as he impacted the ground he awoke. "What the fuck, Doc?" He yelled as his eyelids shot open.

A tsunami size wave of relief crashed over me. I kept him talking to me as I called for additional assistance. I hate the radio. I never know how to talk on that damn thing. Spending my youth watching shows like GI Joe have clearly taught me bad habits and I have a tendency to use terms like "Copy" and "Over" when they are not at all appropriate. Despite my inept military vernacular I managed to get the senior company medic to my location within a matter of minutes. I give him the patient's details and inform him that I need to rally with my platoon; we have been tasked with assaulting a primary target building. He tells me that he can take control of the patient and for me to get to where my guys were now.

I've always been a decent runner, however, running along side an airfield in the middle of the night wearing night vision goggles and about 60 pounds of medical equipment and ammunition tends to affect even the most proficient athletes. The fact that I wasn't entirely sure where I had landed in relation to my platoon's rally point also made things difficult. The cold damp air seized my lungs as my effort increased. The hot breath escaping from my chest was fogging my single green eye-piece. It didn't seem to be helping anyway. Without providing the advantage of depth perception, that night vision device acted more like a luminous green kaleidoscope as it jumped up and down with every impact of my foot to the ground.

As I reach my platoon I am told that a man is down. The Platoon Sergeant tells me that he has sustained a gunshot wound and points to the Ranger lying on his back near a junction box outside of our target building. Seeing a fellow Ranger lying wounded is never an easy thing to take in. This isn't my first experience with it and in the years to come it will become all too familiar. It's not my first time in this scenario but my heart still finds a way to elevate it's already increased tempo after that run. My body feels heavy with the increase of adrenaline and I can feel my limbs become cold as my sympathetic nervous system pulls blood from my extremities. I feel the cold wet grass soak through my pants and kiss my knee immediately as it hits the ground next to Greg. He is alert and answers all of my questions as I sweep his body for holes. He already has a trauma dressing on the wound. I double-check it and a very brief moment of pride sweeps over me because the Ranger I'd taught how to perform immediate tactical combat casualty care did so flawlessly.

Within minutes my Platoon Sergeant is asking me what Greg's status is. My heart rate had found itself in a normal rhythm by this point and I let him know that the patient was stable. I got an 'atta boy' from both Greg and the Sergeant First Class that was standing over me. I'm not sure if it was because I managed to place that massive catheter in his arm in the pitch-black in a matter of seconds or the fact that Greg now realized that the medic has a great deal of autonomy when it comes to dishing out and taking away pain on the battlefield but, he was always a lot nicer to me after that night.

We are given the direction to hit the target building that is a few hundred feet away. I place myself in my Platoon Sergeant's back pocket as we make our way to the entrance. The sharp pop of a flash bang stings my ears as we flow into the poorly lit building. The smell of gunpowder hangs in my nostrils as we move fluidly from room to room. In the darkness of this warehouse gunshots are popping off in controlled pairs from my left and right. No movement requires thinking; everything is instinctual. He goes left. I go right. He moves toward a door. I go through it. We clear the entire warehouse in a matter of minutes. Before I know it we are back outside in the crisp winter air and the sweat that has collected on my cloths creates an inclement environment. We sat like vigilant statues in the darkness. Minutes seemed like hours pulling security on one knee over the building we'd just cleared. Joints become stiff and as the silence played an eerie contrast to the calamity and violence that we had all just experienced. Then that one beautiful word travels through my radio and into my eardrum, "INDEX!"

That means that we are done. This training mission is over. We would conduct a similar training mission each night that week in an effort to ensure that our entire Battalion is prepared for a mass attack on any airport in the world at a moments notice. Sleep would be limited to 3-4 hours per night and the conditions made as close to the real world as possible. The lessons learned from this and the literally hundreds of other training missions that we conducted would be invaluable throughout the course of my time as a

Ranger medic fighting in the Global War on Terrorism.

......

## Chapter 2 - The Hard Sell

John Stuart Mill said, "War is an ugly thing, but not the ugliest of things. The decayed and degraded state of moral and patriotic feeling which thinks that nothing is worth war is much worse. The person who has nothing for which he is willing to fight, nothing which is more important than his own personal safety, is a miserable creature and has no chance of being free unless made and kept so by the exertions of better men than himself."

I discovered that gem after I left the military but somehow it captures the precise emotion that I felt prior to joining the United States Army. I was 20 years old at the time and had been a firefighter for a small department in central Arizona for a little while. I loved my job; it was all I ever wanted to do since I was six years old and saw my father pull up in front of our house in Glendale riding in the back of a giant shiny fire engine. I was beyond lucky to have been hired at such a young age. I graduated high school early so I could attend an EMT course at Glendale Community College. I missed walking at my graduation ceremony because I was helping pull glass out of a man's arm at Thunderbird hospital as a part of my final training to become an emergency medical technician. I was accepted into the fire academy at 18 years old and was one of, if not the youngest member of my class. I loved the academy; it was my first time being a part of a paramilitary organization. The group physical training (PT) was something that I enjoyed very much.  There was also a deep sense of teamwork and camaraderie that I reveled in.  My single father essentially raised me in a fire station.  He worked two jobs to keep my two sisters and myself in decent living conditions.  That man set a shining example of what a parent should be, what a man should be taking on the responsibility of both parents and shouldering more than his share of the task.  Watching him absorb such a burden to ensure that my siblings and I were always taken care of taught me a lesson about responsibility that resonates to this day.  I saw all firefighters that way, benevolent and strong, capable of taking care of their own and putting others needs before their own.

I woke up on my 19th birthday and went for a run before heading off to my academy class.  There was nothing else to eat in my house so I sat down to a tuna fish sandwich for breakfast, turned on the TV as I ate and searched for my boots.  I looked up at the TV just in time to see the second plane strike the World Trade Center.  At the time, the gravity of what happened hadn't sunk in.  It was just another event thousands of miles away being reported on the news.  It didn't seem to have an immediate impact on what I was doing so I pressed on.  I finished my sandwich and headed off to class.  By the time that I arrived the reports of firefighters being trapped in the buildings were already coming in.  The word somber does nothing to describe the mood at the academy that morning.  It was as if every man in that room lost a brother.  They had.  I remembered years earlier when a news report came on TV about a Phoenix firefighter that had been trapped in a building and lost his life.  Even at a young age I saw how much it impacted my father.  The loss of a single fellow firefighter was devastating, whether you were on the same crew or not.  Now we are getting reports of hundreds being killed.  We were let go for the day to be with our families.  The tone was no less melancholy when I got to my father's home.

      It wasn't until months later that the greatest impact of this event hit me.  I had the job that I dreamed of since I was playing with matchbox cars in the sand box behind my house but it didn't feel right.  I saw video images of American's my age preparing to go overseas every day.  These teenagers were getting ready to go to a foreign land to protect my American dream and me.  They didn't know my family or me but they were preparing to place themselves in harms way so that I could continue my version of the American dream.  I stood by everything I loved but this was still incredibly unsettling to me.  It is a difficult feeling to put into words but I guess you could say that I felt like a hypocrite.  Why should I get to sit back for the next 20 years wrapped in a cape of freedom and security that has been provided to me by the exertions of better men than myself.  The decision to join the military was an easy one for me at this point.  The difficult part would be telling my father.

I knew how proud he was of me that I was following in his footsteps.  I know that he would be proud of me no matter what but I almost felt as if it was an insult to leave the very profession that had provided a home and food to me for my entire life.  A part of me felt like I was turning my back on those guys that looked out for me on the job.

When it came time to let my father know what I had decided he responded exactly like I figured that he would.  He was concerned yet supportive.  He has always had my back in everything that I have ever done.  Everything.  I know that he didn't want me to go into the military, especially since our country was going to be fighting a war on two different fronts.  He put that aside and got me in touch with a former Air Force Special Operations Pararescuemen - PJ.  At the time I was planning on going in as a combat medic.  Bob, the PJ, told me, "there is only one place in the Army for a hard charging swinging dick like (me).... that's the Rangers."  He said, "You can be a medic if you want, that's cool, but do it with the Rangers."

I respected Bob; hell, I still respect him.  He let me come to his home where he shared pictures and stories from his time in special operations.  It made me incredibly excited for the challenge ahead. I owe a part of my success to the advice that Bob gave me during that time.  Having a former member of special operations as a mentor was invaluable to my success.  Pieces of advice like, "be the grey man" would echo through my thoughts throughout my training.

......

# Chapter 3 - FAR

I can't feel my hands. Why the hell can't we put our hands in our pockets? What is the point of putting pockets in the uniform if it is against the rules to put your hands in them? It's late November 2003, the first day of Ranger Indoctrination Program or RIP for short. Even the name suggests that we are all in for a near-death experience. I have already graduated from Army basic training, Army Combat medic school and Airborne school to get here.

There are 150 of us standing in formation waiting for the madness to begin. There was close to 500 in our RIP-hold group. There were simply too many guys coming out of Airborne school and not enough equipment for them to start a class. Every month the top 150 physical agility scores got spots to the next RIP class, the rest would roll back into a holding pattern that some say is worse than RIP itself. The PT test is nothing special, it consists of 2 minutes of max effort push ups, 2 minutes of max effort sit ups and a 2 mile run.

There really isn't an agenda so while waiting to get into the next class we would get tasked out to anyone on post that needed something done. We would pull weeds, get smoked, paint curbs, get smoked, move furniture, get smoked, change targets at shooting ranges, get smoked, stand around in formation for hours on end, and then you guessed it, get smoked.  Getting smoked is an interesting occurrence.  The first time it happens is very confusing.  I recall being in a sort of holding barracks before starting basic training and some guy decided to take a nap.  The drill Sergeant made the entire group do push ups.  As soon as the majority of guys couldn't do push ups anymore he had us roll to our backs and do flutter kicks until we failed at that.  This went on for about 15 minutes or so.  The entire time I couldn't help but think, why the fuck am I getting punished because this asshole was on his neck in the middle of the day?   I would come to learn that there were varying degrees of "getting smoked."  There was the quick, "we got shit to do but you were being dumb so do 25 push ups and get up" smoking.  There was the, "I'm trying to teach you a lesson that will help you survive the rigors of combat" smoking. There was the, "I know I can make this kid quit if I make him do air squats until he pukes on himself" smoking. There was the "Fuck you I just got my Ranger tab or my promotion so I'm going to mess you up because I've been getting messed up every day for the last 2 years" smoking. And my personal favorite the, "I don't even have a reason, I'm just fucking board and I out-rank you so start doing push ups" smoking.

These torture sessions included movements that would make your CrossFit workout seem like a trip to day camp.  Things like "little man in the woods" and "8 count body builders" or my personal favorite the "yes-no-maybe."  As bad as getting screamed at while doing hundreds if not thousands of repetitions of various calisthenics was, the worst was being made to stand in one place without moving for hours at a time. The throbbing that occurs in your joints after an Ironman pales in comparison to standing motionless on concrete all day.

One Friday while in RIP hold, our cadre partial emerged from a window in front of our formation and called for a private. Five guys from the front row ran over immediately. Of course he didn't ask for five, he asked for one, so we all got smoked. "RECOVER" the cadre shouts and we stand up. "You, you, you and you, get the fuck back in formation. YOU, I will let this entire formation go home if you can sing a Britney Spears song right now!" The guy panics, not wanting the 400+ guys in front of him think that he knows lyrics to a Britney Spears song. "3...2....1. Chance is up, get back in line asshole! Looks like none of you are going home anytime soon," shouts the cadre. He shuts the window to return to his nice warm office. Thirty minutes later he emerges once again. This time he singles out one guy, "You! Get up here and sing me a Britney song or so help me God I will leave you all out here all fucking night!"

"BABY BABY HOW WAS I SUPPOSED TO KNOW...."

"HAHA Help him out fuckers!" He yelled from the window. The collective voice of 400 wannabe Army Rangers echoed out the words to that song.  By this point the Staff Sergeant in the window was laughing uncontrollably and can hardly get the words out, "Get the fuck out of here, all of you!" We scatter like roaches when the lights come on.  NO ONE wants to be stuck in that place a minute longer than they have to. I made the mistake of hanging out in the barracks on my first weekend in Pre-RIP.  I ended up spending two days picking up shell casings at a range and setting up targets for a group of guys in Battalion. You want to talk about getting smoked, try being a Pre-RIP student on a weekend detail with a bunch of Rangers.  I never made that mistake again.  A couple of friends and I would get a hotel room just off post and spend our weekends sleeping and writing the Ranger creed hundreds of times. To be honest most guys failed the PT test on purpose so they wouldn't have to endure RIP after all of this torture.  The ironic thing was that the guys who failed intentionally would be there twice as long while they were getting placed with other units.

By the first day of Ranger Indoc I had been in the Army for about eight months.  Falling into a formation was second nature.  You have to make sure that you are directly behind the man in front of you and directly between the men to your right and left.  Everyone is organized by their last name to make roll call go faster.  It has to look pretty or you are going to pay by way of physical abuse.  The first morning of RIP everyone made sure to be in place early to ensure that our formation was squared away. We stood in the cold, damp Georgia darkness for what felt like hours awaiting the first day to begin. My fingers are numb from the cold and despite standing still for so long, I could still hear the heartbeats of the men around me pounding out in a collective concern for what was about to happen. We are standing on what feels like sacred ground, the walls around us have the accolades from every major battle that the 75th Ranger Regiment had been involved in and beneath our feet was what had simply come to be known as "the blacktop." This ground has seen more sweat than the floor of a child labor camp in communist China. This blacktop has taken away more men's dreams than the act of poking a hole in a condom. We stand facing an old white barracks building with chipping paint and cracked walls that used to house the members of 3rd Ranger Battalion before the new compound was built. It now housed all of us Ranger-wannabes.

The large double doors swing open and as much as we want to look at who is coming out, we know better. From the corner of my eye I catch a glimpse of him. The man that emerged was daunting figure who I will call Staff Sergeant Runza. He was easily 215 pounds and stood over six feet tall. It was 5 o'clock in the morning but his entire bottom lip was packed to the gills with chewing tobacco. Runza had a clipboard in his hands with our class roster. He gave us the simple instruction that he would call off our last name and we would sound off with our first name and middle initial. The process was going smoothly until he got to my friend, Lewis. Runza called off, "Lewis!"

"Lewis" he responded.

"Your first name asshole!"

"Lewis, Sergeant" he shouted once again.

At this time Runza rushed to where Lewis was standing and got in his face. He looked at his nametape, it said 'Lewis'. The entire class could feel how pissed off our new instructor was, the groups collective heart rate elevated as his anger was palpable. He grabbed Lewis by the collar giving him one last chance to follow the instruction. "What is your first name, asshole?" he screamed.

"Lewis, Sergeant"

"Your father named you Lewis Lewis?"

"Roger Sergeant"

"You have got to be kidding me!! What kind of asshole names his kid the same thing twice? What is your father's name?"

"Lewis, Sergeant"

"No fucking way! No Goddamn way! Please tell me you don't have kids Lewis Lewis!"

"Roger Sergeant, I do"

"So help me God Lewis Lewis, if you named your poor bastard Lewis I am going to punch you square in the fucking mouth!"

"Negative Sergeant, I have two girls"

"Even God knew the insanity had to stop! Now get the fuck down!"

Lewis began knocking out push-ups as Runza continued through the roll call.  This would not be our last encounter with Runza.  At one point during RIP he told our class that he would take us out into the woods, every one of us, and end our pathetic lives.  I believed with all my heart that he could do it, that he was capable of killing 150 men barehanded.

The first major event following the PT test in RIP is the Combat Water Survival Test (CWST).  It isn't anything too terribly difficult, they just want to make sure that you are not afraid of the water.  One of the events has the men blindfolded and walking off of a 10-foot high dive.  The cadre would be behind the soldier guiding them to the end.  We were instructed to yell "RANGER" and jump.  I witnessed one of the poor bastards that hesitated at the moment of truth.  Runza had a fist full of the back of his BDU top, standing behind him on that high dive.  It was a sort of push, pull maneuver that he used.  The push was to force that kid off the diving board, the pull was to ensure that he wasn't going to hit feet first!  All I heard was his mangled attempt at calling out "RANGER," which sounded more like "RAMMMFER" as his back impacted the water with the force of a Mac truck hitting a fucking watermelon.

The next two days were filled with constant smoke sessions and a timed 5-mile run that everyone was required to complete, in formation, in under 40 minutes.  One unfortunate wannabe

Ranger lost his shoe somewhere around mile three and ran the remaining two miles with one shoe! When the cadre saw the kid standing in formation with one shoe and one very bloody sock after the run they smoked him for being stupid and not stopping to grab his shoe. He asked, "Sergeant, I wouldn't have met the standard and been dropped from the course if I had gone back."

The cadre responded, "Oh yeah, you would have been let go, but you're still a fucking idiot!"

The big gut check during RIP is a three-day field training exercise at Cole Range on Fort Benning. All that you really know going into it is that you will be doing land navigation at some point and an 8-mile road march at the end. Neither of these events would be too difficult without the compound stress of being on the move constantly with very little, if any sleep for the days leading up to them. I learned something about myself over those 72 hours. A lesson that I still draw from to this day; I like seeing other people quit. I'm not sure how many people quit that first night - maybe 20? Maybe 30? Maybe more. It was an enticing notion as we did flutter kicks and push-ups in the ankle deep freezing puddles that accumulated from the constant downpour of sleet and icy rain. Just quit and you will be warm. The cadre made this choice much easier for many of the men by standing around a giant campfire cooking hot dogs. They took turns leaving the warmth of their bonfire to come torture us throughout the evening. We were out in an open field and I believe that evening was the first time that I ever heard the command, "Hit the woodline!"

Everyone started running for the woods, so I followed along. I don't like being second at anything so I sprinted the 200 meters round trip to ensure that I would be the first one back. That's not a good idea. Don't do that. Don't ever be the first guy back. I messed up my mentors number one rule, be the grey man. I just spotlighted myself.

The cadre asked where his favorite stick was.

"Pardon Sergeant?" I replied.

"You went all the way to the woodline and didn't bring me my favorite stick back?? GO GET MY FAVORITE STICK ASSHOLE!!"

"Roger Sergeant!" It was a response that I had been programmed to give by this point; it was the only way that I could reply. So as the rest of the guys were running back to the circle of pain and I was running back to the woodline to find homeboys favorite stick. Can you guess how many times it took to find his favorite stick? I'll give you a hint... it wasn't on the first fucking trip!

It sucks. It all sucks, but that's the point. Your legs are filled with concrete and your lungs don't feel like expanding even one more time. The freezing air has penetrated your joints rendering them crippled. At 20 years old you get a glimpse into the future, you see what it is going to be like to be 80. You feel frail and broken. The simple truth is that it is just as miserable for you as it is for every other beaten down guy out there so when he quits and you keep going, you know that you are mentally stronger than he is and that is something that you can't buy. I welcome this pain beating down on me. That builds a confidence that you will walk with until your dying day. That is the difference between being a Ranger or a SEAL or any other member of special operations. Day in and day out you get to work with a group of guys that didn't quit when things got tough and that is invaluable.

Just because you get through Cole Range doesn't mean that you are going to be getting a tan beret handed to you. There are still two more weeks of events designed to weed candidates out. (Ranger selection is now an 8-week process but I went through it back when it was so hard that they got the job done in less than half the time.) The 12-mile road march at the time required each man to be within arms reach of the man in front of him. No running was allowed. In fact I watched a couple of guys get spear tackled into the woods for running to keep up. The 12-miler got a lot of people for that reason. We had tests on Ranger history and combat lifesaving techniques. Each time that you passed an event you could feel yourself getting closer to achieving the goal. We kept a mental countdown the way a nine year old does as Christmas draws nearer.

We were on lock down one Sunday. The few dozen remaining members of our RIP class were cleaning things that had long ago been made spotless, waiting for the next round or torture. As I polished my boots for the 3rd time I remembered that in basic training if we chose to go to church that they had to release us. I told my good friend Jess about my plan to escape for a few hours by telling the staff duty officer that I wished to attend Sunday services. Jess and I had first met in basic training. He was a great athlete who played soccer in college before joining the Army. Since he had a degree he had automatically been promoted to Specialist, E4. His shaved head hid the fact that he had very curly dark hair. His demeanor always reminded me of Matthew McConaughey in the way that everything was cool. No matter how bad we were getting crushed, Jess just took it with a grin.

Unbeknownst to me some kid overheard our conversation and asked to tag along. I knew that if more people found out it wouldn't happen. There is no way that they are going to let 40 of us leave. We told him to keep his mouth shut about it and he could come. We head downstairs to ask permission to leave and who is the staff duty? Yup, Staff Sergeant Runza! Fuck. My. Life.

He wasn't in uniform. He was sitting with his feet kicked up on the desk in a wife beater and jeans watching TV. His fingers were interlaced behind his head exposing the tattoos on the insides of his biceps. One of which was a Catholic nun, spread eagle with her genitals pierced, of course the jewelry dangling from her lady parts was a gold cross. What else would it be?

I attempted to muster up as much courage as I had to ask permission to go to religious services. He barely glanced at us and replied, "I don't give a fuck."

As we turn to leave the kid does something I couldn't believe. He stops and asks Runza, "Sergeant, what service should we be going to?"

I can only compare that feeling to that moment when you see the red and blue lights spinning behind you after you ran a red light and you know you are fucked! Except this guy wasn't going to issue us a ticket, he was going to put our skulls through the brick wall. Runza's attention is taken from the TV for the first time as he leans forward, spits a wad of tobacco into the trashcan and says, "Do I look like someone who knows when church starts? Do I look like a mother fucker that believes in GOD?"

How do you answer that question? Fuck no he doesn't; but I'm not going to say that to him. Luckily he was staring at homeboy that asked the question but we knew that we were just as much on the hook just for being with him. The kid began to shake a little and replied, "I don't think so Sergeant." Now, that's the wrong answer. Thinking and being in RIP are two diametrically opposed things. Tell him, no, negative, roger, hell tell him to go fuck himself but don't say some dumb shit like "I don't THINK so."

To be honest I'm not sure how we made it out of there alive. I'll tell you one thing, that kid did not graduate!  We ditched him the moment we left the barracks.  The closest church was only a quarter mile away and we didn't have any desire to walk a step further than necessary.  Never in all my days did I think that I would have attended a full on choir singing Baptist ceremony where my friend and myself were the only two white people in attendance.  It was like a scene from a movie.  We rolled into that place in our tattered grey Army PT uniform with tan lines around our shaved heads marking where our patrol caps sat even with the marching surface (in accordance with AR 670-1 of course) to be greeted by some of the sharpest dressed, singing, clapping group of people you have ever come across.  We were so out of place that we couldn't help but laugh at ourselves.  It was a much-needed comedic relief before returning to the harsh world of special operations selection.

We had made it through the jump training and fast roping, the sleepless nights and the constant physical abuse.  We endured the gut wrenching torture that comes from being told that today is "all you can eat day" in the chow hall after being in the field for days without a hot meal only to be given two minutes to consume all of the food on our plates.  The run back to the company area following that trap had to have been at least a 6-minute mile pace.  Jess survived scoring the only goal on our cadre during "combat soccer" although he paid a terrible price for juking Runza.

All of that was over now; we were graduating. We would be receiving our Ranger scroll and tan beret on a freezing cold December morning. As we recited the 242-word Ranger creed in unison on graduation the collective breath of around 40 brand new Rangers filled the air like smoke clouds leaving a wild fire. We were about to become the most elite soldiers in the U.S. Army, or so we thought.

From Left to right; Jess, me, Adam, Chris. On the day that we graduated RIP.

....

# Chapter 4 - The Running Free

Typically being in a holdover status in the military is the absolute worst place to be, it's purgatory. Since you don't have an official job you get tasked to do all the tedious remedial bullshit that no one else will. There was a small group of medics that had recently graduated from Ranger Indoc that were now 'Real Rangers' Instead of a job we had an open ended wait ahead of us for our next school. Unlike Medic and Airborne school, there were very limited spaces for Rangers in the Special Operations Medic Course (SOMC). I recognized several of the guys who I was reporting to the Regiment with but a few were strangers.

I first met Matt in basic training but didn't really get to know him until our first day reporting to the 75th Ranger Regiment. We were the final RIP class of 2003 and had a couple of weeks leave for Christmas immediately after graduating. There were apparently nine medics in our RIP class that graduated.

On the morning that we were to report there were only eight of us there. Again, I didn't know Matt that well at the time so the fact that he just signed his own death warrant didn't bother me beyond the fact that the rest of us would no doubt be getting scuffed up until he returned. To my utter shock, Specialist Fabra, who was immediately in charge of the nine of us, wasn't pissed. He didn't drop any of us, even when I made the nervous error of calling him Sergeant.  Over the past ten months of our training it was very uncommon to have someone other than a Sergeant in charge so referring to him as such came very naturally.  The other seven guys in the room looked at me with contempt, as I'm sure they all believed that my error would soon become their burden.  That's how it works in the military, if you fuck up EVERYONE pays for it.  It is a good analogy for combat, and an effective way of weeding out those that cannot effectively work as a team.

This time was different though; Matt showed up to Georgia two days later and was never reprimanded.  I would find out later that he was stuck in Chicago due to a massive snowstorm and I would find out even later that this guy could get away with shit that no other person I have ever known could get away with.  He is currently in medical school and has threatened to sue me if I tell any of these stories about him. But fuck him; these stories need to be told.

To my surprise, our time waiting for a slot to SOMC was actually pretty fun.  We had an early formation, did PT, helped organize medical supplies and lifted weights.  More often than not we were released by 14:00 and given long weekends because command didn't know what to do with us.  With the exception of one or two guys acting stupid and getting their brand new scrolls cut off, the time we spent at Regiment was actually quite enjoyable.  We took full advantage of the long weekends and traveled as much as our budgets would allow. I was one of two in the group who had recently purchased a vehicle so I was almost always at the center of the debauchery.

"232. 232...232," he mumbled for the fifth time. Some fucking navigator you are Jess, we've been off of 232 for twenty miles. And damn it, if you throw up in my new truck I will kick you out here at the Florida border.

It's January 2004, Jess and I had been looking out for each other (read competing with each other) since about the first day of basic training. What we had been through already would pale in comparison to what we would eventually go through but we already had a pretty inseparable bond. Even so, if he throws up in my truck I will not hesitate to punch him right in the .... and there it goes, vomit everywhere!

We had a four-day weekend and I had just bought an extended cab truck. I'm not sure exactly whose idea it was but someone suggested taking a road trip from Ft. Benning, Georgia down to Panama City, Florida. I had never really gone on a real road trip before and I jumped at the opportunity. I went online and found an inexpensive hotel on the beach, booked it and started packing. There was just enough room in my little truck for Matt, Jess, Chris and myself. As we left the gates of the military installation, Matt yells, "Pull over, pull over!!"

"What, why?"

"You can't have a road trip without some booze now can you?"

Brandishing a very large bottle of Jack Daniels, Matt exits the liquor store with a grin that would make the Cheshire cat from Alice in Wonderland proud. Chris was only 20 at the time and had a striking resemblance to Opie Taylor from the Andy Griffith Show. He was a quiet guy, not unlike myself at the time. Our two travel partners for the weekend, however, were anything but. Like Jess, Matt also had a college degree so they both had a few years of drinking experience on Chris and myself.

Those three went through that bottle like Kobayashi goes through hot dogs. We had to stop at another liquor store within an hour. By the time that we were in Florida they were passed the point of being helpful. Matt and Chris were in the back beating the snot out of one another and Jess just lost his Arby's all over the front seat of my truck. I learned a valuable lesson about taking road trips that weekend; don't be the only sober one. I manage to find the hotel using an outdated map and despite the lack of assistance from my friends. I was pretty pissed by the time that we got to the hotel but the site of the ocean washed all that away, "PANAMA CITY BABY!!"

This was going to be amazing! All I knew about Panama City was what I had seen on MTV Spring Break. After nearly a year of straight Army training surrounded by nothing but other guys, we were all ready for college girls in bikinis!

As we enter the lobby we notice a table of senior citizens playing cards. We walk out to the pool and it's a ghost town. The beach was equally deserted. We go inside to check in. In as surly a tone as any I've ever heard, Matt asks the older women behind the desk, "Where the hell are all the women at?"

She looked at the group of us with curiosity and then explained that in the winter most of the hotels are rented as time-shares to snowbirds.

Jaws. Floor.

Not sure why all four of us assumed that there would be wet t-shirt contests and body shots going on in January. SHIT! We did not think this one through very well. What is it those Marines say? Improvise, adapt and overcome?

The first night was a little irritating. We drove around looking for a place that could serve our function, the closest we could find was a Hooters. The high point of that experience was watching Jess be refused service because he was already so unbelievable wasted.

We woke up late the next morning and decided that we needed to find breakfast. We drove around but all that we could find was some shit hole Chinese buffet. When we sat down Matt immediately ordered a double Jack and Coke.

"For breakfast, really?"

"Fuck it!" was his only response.

Matt sucked down at least three of those before we were asked to leave. Not sure if you've ever been kicked out of a buffet before noon but if you get the chance I say go for it!  Matt's technique involved a constant stream of obscenities at a decibel level similar to that of a fire truck.  We drove around for a while and found a place that had a bunch of motorcycles out front.  Knowing that a group of drunken bikers would be our best chance for some decent trouble, we immediately pulled over and went inside.  I had never seen anything like it!  It was literally a bar in the middle of a liquor store! I mean, you could order a shot and then turn around and grab a case of PBR from the shelf behind you.

Matt quickly discovered a drink that they called "hunch punch."  God only knows what was in that concoction but the leather-skinned old biker lady behind the bar said that she had never seen anyone drink more than two and be able to walk out the door on their own.

Matt, of course, took this as a challenge.  He was on his third one when he started talking shit to some of the bikers.  Not wanting to wear out our welcome, or get our teeth knocked in, we decided it would be a good time to abscond.  In an act of sheer defiance, Matt downs the remaining contents of his third libation and struts out the door.  We quickly find another bar that looks promising.  On the front is a sign that says "Fog Horn Leg Horn's." As we walk to the front door I proclaim, "I say, I say son.... let's get toasted."

Matt bellies up to the bar while Chris and I shoot pool. The bartender is a beautiful blonde girl in her early twenties. Jess turns on that Matthew McConaughey charm immediately. I'm not surprised at all that she is smitten with him, Jess always had that thing that women found interesting. He was a Kansas boy with a big smile and always seemed to be interested in whatever you had to say. He used his skills to quickly find out where all the locals spent their free time. I missed most of what was said due to the fact that I was getting my ass handed to me on the pool table by a 20 year old ginger. The conversation must have turned political in some way because in the middle of that nearly empty bar Matt stood up on his stool and screamed, "You're a Democrat? FUCK YOU!"

Here's the thing about screaming curse words at a pretty girl in a bar, if you're going to do it, don't fall off of your bar stool immediately afterward. That will make you look like twice the asshole!

As we pick Matt up off the floor we apologize profusely to everyone in the bar including the little old lady that was sitting a few bar stools down. As her wrinkled hand brings the ultra slim to her mouth, she tells us that we might want to get our friend under control. We prop him back on his barstool and get him water. Matt spits on the floor and the elderly woman explains that he shouldn't do that. He asks, "oh yeah, why not?" She responds, "well because this is my bar, I own in and I don't appreciate it."

Matt's eyes open widely for the first time in hours. I believe that a normal person's reaction would have been, 'oh shit, I've been acting like an ass in front of the owner this entire time.' Not. Even. Close. Matt gets off of his bar stool, stumbles over to her, sits down next to granny Clampit, and starts hitting on her! I'm not making this up. He proceeds to confirm that all of the booze behind the bar belongs to her and starts talking her up. Surprisingly, she seems unfazed by the whole thing. She just smiles and takes another drag. Without warning or provocation Matt falls off of his bar stool for a second time, flat on his back. A roar of laughter escaped him as he lay on the floor.

"He should go," says the old bar owner.

"Yeah. That's not a bad idea," said Chris.

As we walk to my truck, Matt decides to unzip and micturate without missing a step. Just a grown ass man walking through a parking lot actively urinating - no big deal. As he attempts to climb into the cab of my truck I yell, "OHH FUCK NO! Your piss covered self isn't getting into my new truck! Jess already puked in there, you ride in the back!" Chris laughed but what he didn't realize was that he was going to have to ride back there and keep him from jumping out.

"Hey look," said Jess as I started the truck, "It's only 6:30."

As we got back to the retirement center, the effects of those "hunch punch" drinks really began to take their full effect. Matt attempted to jump off of the fourth floor balcony a half a dozen times before we even got to our room. Jess and I utilized some of our Army medic skills and did a two-person buddy carry back to the room. Chris opens the hideous aqua colored door and we take Matt to the bed. We throw him face down onto the mattress. Like a plank he bounces off and hits the floor. Fed up with his antics, none of us bother to move him. We walk to the kitchenette area, that's when we heard it: a shrill cry that I would come to know as an indicator that Matt was past the point of reasoning. This was the first time that I heard him yell, "I DO WHAT I WANT! "

He went from dead on the floor to full sprint in an instant, like some kind of undead in a cheesy zombie movie. To this day I have no idea what that clown was thinking as he sprinted, full speed, face first into that closed aqua door. He bounced like a fucking pinball, spinning just slightly and then striking the back of his head on the bathroom doorframe. One complete, standing 360-degree spin, and SMACK, the back of his head hits the tile floor.

"Ohh shit!" Chris yells, "That's a lot of blood!"

In an effort to preserve Matt's political career I am choosing to leave out the stream of obscenities that flowed from his mouth as I attempted to put pressure on the back of his split dome. To be honest the concern was more for my deposit than the back of his head. I didn't want him spraying blood all over the carpet. It took about 15 minutes to calm him down.

Before Matt's egregious verbal assault on our beautiful bartender, Jess managed to gather a valuable piece of Intel. We now know where the locals will be tonight. The only problem is our good friend just busted the back of his head open and could very easily have a concussion, add that to the amount of alcohol that he has coursing through his veins and leaving him alone could mean big trouble. There was only one honorable thing to do: leave Chris with Matt's drunk ass while Jess and I go try to find some mischief.

In Ranger Battalion, when a shitty task has to get done and everyone is the same rank we revert to "Time In Battalion" or "TIB." Chris wasn't as excited about our plan as we were but we explained to him that he was the youngest of the group and hence had the least or "Time In Life" or "TIL."

"Can't believe he went for that," said Jess as we left the hotel room in search of a night of trouble.

"Uggghhh, what happened?" moaned Matt as the sun snuck in through the blinds and attacked his eyes. "What the... why's my head stuck to the sheet?"

Laughter fills the room as Chris says, "Matt.... dude... You're an idiot!"

We are all slow moving for the first few minutes. Matt finally discovers the paper clip size gash on the back of his head and asks again, "Seriously, what the fuck happened? Did one of you ass clowns hit me with something?"

We all take an almost sadistic level of pleasure in telling him the story. I take a look at the now swollen mess and decide that maybe he should get stitches. "Do you know how to do that?" He asks. I lie through my teeth and say yes. Suturing is a skill that we would all become very skilled at but at this point none of us had attended Special Operations Medical Course. We had all graduated from Army Combat Medic School about six months before but the scope of practice is as different as an E.M.T. to a Physician's Assistant.

We decide to take care of Matt's wounds instead of going to the beach, which was probably the single responsible decision that was made in that 96-hour period. A stink cloud of booze and shame lingers on us like Pig Pen from Charlie Brown as we enter the CVS. I am wearing a dirty grey tank top and am clearly still a little drunk from the night before. We begin to rummage through the medical supplies isle. Concerned I'm sure, the pharmacist emerges from behind the counter to ask if we need assistance. I ask her in a very calm matter where we could find the "at home suture kits." "Excuse me," she replies as if this is the first time someone has ever asked such a question. "What on earth do would you need that for?" she asks.

"Hey Matt! Come here!"

When he emerges from the next aisle over, I have him spin around and show the attractive twenty something brunette in the short white lab coat the extent of his injuries. Her tan skin turns a pale shade of green as she covers her mouth. The site of the swollen, half crusted yet still bleeding scalp must have been a bit more than she had bargained for. Without blinking she begins to shake her head and say, "We.... we.... wouldn't have anything like that here."

"Hmmmm, well then.... can you tell me where the fishing line and hooks might be?"

"GET OUT! All of you, get out!"

"Okay then."

We stumble back to the parking lot feeling slightly defeated. As we look to our right the beams of golden light shine down from the heavens on the building next to CVS. The sign reads, "Kwicker Liquor." We look at each other and all have the exact same thought at the exact same time.

"Sooooo you guys wanna just get fucked up?"

"Sounds good!"

We roll into this place with the verve of a pack of nine year olds entering a Toys-R-US! Except for Chris, he was only twenty so we made him wait in the truck.  We emerged victoriously with two 30 racks of liquid gold. Pabst. Blue. Ribbon.  "This should get us through the morning, what do you think Chris?"

I'm not going to lie to you; the rest of that weekend is a little blurry.  I do recall, however, Chris pulling the most clutch move I have ever seen a 20 year old pull off in a bar.  He somehow danced his way into the center ring of the entire girls water polo team from University of Arizona.  They were in Florida for a tournament, or at least that is the story that they told us.  They invited us to watch their next game in two days in Tallahassee.  Chris got their numbers and we actually managed to meet up with them after their game. As the other three men on that trip are all now happily married I will omit the details of the remainder of that evening out of respect for their wives.  I will say that getting to shave Matt's laced open head before formation on Monday was a real treat. That wound should have definitely received stitches.  Years later at his wedding he would retell the story and showed me the massive scar that he still has.

Escorting Matt to our hotel room

Hanging out with the girls water polo team

.....

Panama City was our first long weekend trip of our holdover time at Regiment but there was several others that were just as memorable. We had a long weekend on Valentine's Day and Jess invited us to go back home to Kansas with him. Since a big reason why I joined the military was to see new places, I naturally jumped at the opportunity.  Once again Jess, Matt, Chris and myself were set free to have our way with an unsuspecting city.  Jess had been dating the same girl back home for awhile and for some reason thought that having her be our designated driver on Valentine's Day weekend was a good idea.  Of course we weren't going to try to talk him out of it, we were just hopeful that she had a few morally casual friends that wanted to hang out.  The first few nights were pretty status quo.  We spent the bulk of our meager months pay on bar tabs and junk food at 2am.  Valentine's Day was the final evening that we were in town.  Someone must have talked some sense into Jess because he decided to leave us at his friend's house with a couple cases of beer while he took his girlfriend out to dinner.  This would have been a smart move except we were told that his friend had a new female roommate that wasn't currently home.

The two cases of Bud Light were just enough to get us riled up.  I'm pretty sure that Matt and I tried to fight each other in the living room.  Chris broke us up and I went into the bathroom to cool down.  When I was in there I noticed a shadow box filled with various sailor knots.  It seemed to me that the bowline was not done correctly so I felt the need to tie everything in that bathroom that was long enough into the proper bowline.  Lucky for me this girl that I had never met had several curling irons, hair dryers and other electronic devices with long cords.  When I ran out of things to tie I began rearranging everything that wasn't bolted down into a giant pyramid. I must have been in that bathroom for an hour. By the time I stumbled out Matt and Chris had already passed out on the couches in the living room. I decided that my best course of action would be to pass out naked in front of the mystery girl's bedroom door in anticipation of her arrival. Don't bother trying to understand the cognitive process of a 21-year-old Ranger private with over 20 beers on board.

Unbeknownst to me, blondie came home while I was in the middle of destroying her bathroom. I didn't find this out until I heard a very loud scream coming from her room and she ran out, tripping over me. Apparently Matt had wandered into her bedroom mistaking it for the latrine and commenced relieving himself on the keyboard to her desktop computer. When she screamed, "WHAT THE FUCK ARE YOU DOING? WHO ARE YOU?" Matt replied with, "Don't worry, I'm Jess' buddy." Now, she had never met Jess before. In fact she had just moved in within the last month. So in under a minute she is startled awake by one guy pissing on her Dell, trips over another guy naked in her doorway and flees to her bathroom for refuge to find the whole fucking place tied into bowline knots. Needless to say we were not invited back. I heard she moved out soon after.

......

## Chapter 5 - Cuts Marked in the March of Men

       The fun and games of holdover would have to come to an end so the fun and games of Special Operations Medic School could commence.

       "MEDIC!!!"

       I hear the scream from within the woodline. This is it, the final practical hands on exam for trauma lanes for Special Operations Medical Course (SOMC). This is the culmination of months of comprehensive hands on training and 40 hours a week in a classroom. The next 30 minutes will determine whether or not I get to advance on to the one-month clinical rotation or I get washed out. There are 300 points total, of which there are a handful of immediate disqualifiers or "No-Go's" if missed. We have been going over this sequence for weeks in the woods of Fort Bragg, North Carolina. Every possible scenario, every imaginable injury has been covered by our instructors, guys that have been operating as Special Ops medics for years.

       The first three months of the course is focused heavily on didactics. We go through anatomy, physiology, pathology, kinesiology, pharmacology and every other "ology" there is. I laughed on the first day when the instructor said that this course would be like trying to drink from a fire hose. It didn't take long to figure out what he meant. The amount of information that we were responsible for learning was incredible. It wasn't abnormal to have three or four tests on the same day. It was equivalent to taking 60 college credits in 6 months.

The attrition rate is one of the highest of any school in the military. Every guy here had previously passed a rigorous physical test; it was an eclectic mix of bad asses. The majority of our class was comprised of guys in the "Q-course" who had passed Special Forces selection and were en route to getting their Green Beret. If they successfully passed this course they would still have to complete several other phases of training before receiving their Special Forces tab and Green Beret. There were about a half a dozen Seals that had just endured six months of BUDs, and a handful of Marine Recon Corpsman that had to pass Recon selection. There were about a half a dozen Rangers in our class, all guys that I had gotten to know pretty well during our time as holdovers after RIP. There were also a couple of members of an Army Civil Affairs unit and two staff sergeants from the Air Force. One of the Air Force members was a female, who, to my knowledge, was the first female to be admitted to any course like this in the military. Additionally, we had a couple of members of Special Forces units from two different countries.

The academic portion had wiped out nearly half of our class. If they were deemed to be "trainable" they would recycle and have the opportunity to start again.

Before we get to trauma lanes we lose a couple more class members during our live tissue labs. This phase of training is what truly separates special operations medics from all of the other pre-hospital medical training programs. This type of training has been seen as controversial due to the outrage by organizations like PETA.

Before we conduct any training on the animals we spend considerable time learning their anatomy. Every precaution is taken so that they feel absolutely no pain or discomfort. We administer a heavy sedative before intubating. From this point forward we were not allowed to refer to the patient as a goat, we were told that they were a 9-year-old child and were to be treated as such. Over the next two weeks I didn't see a single incident that involved the disrespect or abuse of those patients. Every member of our class conducted themselves with the highest degree of professionalism.

The first week was general skills. We were divided into four-man teams. Each team would have it's own patient each day. We would each do a series of four to five surgical procedures starting with the least invasive and working our way to more invasive. We did our best to put into action the procedures that we had practiced on mannequins in the preceding weeks. We made use of the external carotid arteries and used the smaller vessels to practice the venous cut down, which involved cutting and blunt dissecting the tissue around a vein in order to expose it.  This was necessary in the event that peripheral venous access could not be obtained and fluids had to be administered intravenously.  (In a separate live tissue lab years later we learned several forms of interoseous fluid administration techniques on pigs.)  I lost count of the number of surgical cricothyrotomy and tracheostomy's performed.  Tube thoracotomy was also done multiple times per day.  We would finish each day with a hemorrhage lab where an instructor would severe a major artery and we would be responsible for stopping the bleeding.  The ability to perform this skill alone has saved the lives of countless human beings, including enemy combatants.

The following week we would be tested on each of the skills.  Most of the class did well through this phase due largely to the way that the course is taught.  On the last day we take the caprine to the incinerator.  As we are stacking them in, one of the German Special Forces soldiers made the comment that if we stack them a certain way we can fit more in.  Our jaws drop to the floor and Adam, one of the Green Berets who was re-classing from Special Forces weapons Sergeant to Special Forces medical Sergeant, burst out laughing so hard that he literally fell to the ground.  Within an instant the rest of us followed suit.  Tears rolled from my eyes as I tried to catch my breath.  Our 6'4" German friend has no clue why we are laughing.

"What is funny?" he asks earnestly.

"You're fucking joking right?"

"No, what is funny?"

"The German guy giving advice on how to fit more bodies into an incinerator, come on man! Your military has some experience in that kind of thing do they?"

We can see the embarrassment in his eyes. He didn't think about it in that way at all.

He replies, "We don't speak of that time in our history."

"What do you mean you don't speak of it?" asks one of the Seals.

"It is taboo, we don't discuss it."

Not one among us feels bad about busting his balls. Later that night we buy him a beer and continue to joke with him about it. I believe it was his first experience with American soldiers sense of humor.

With live tissue training done it is time to move on to the most physically demanding part of the Special Operations Medic Course. We would spend each day for the next three weeks in the sweltering heat of the North Carolina woods. All of which would culminate in a single thirty-minute assessment of our ability to perform in an austere environment.

I respond to the call for "MEDIC!"

Running about 80 meters into the woods I find my patient laying face-up, covered in fake blood. The trauma management sequence flows from my mouth like the pledge of allegiance did when I was in first grade.  It was burned into my memory.  My hands complete each movement as my mouth describes in detail what I am doing to my instructor who is standing over me with a clipboard.

"BSI, Scene is safe, I have one patient, Haji and I can handle..."

The instructor echoes back, "Scene is safe, you have one patient, no further assistance needed."

"Buddy? Buddy are you okay?"

"Your patient responds with a moan and says it hurts."

"Where does it hurt?

"My chest."

"Do you know where you are?"

"Patient responds, I'm in the woods."

"Do you know your name and rank?"

"Patient responds, Sgt. Smith."

"Do you know how long you've been hurt?

"I've been here for less than ten minutes."

"Patient is alert and oriented to person, place and time"

I check for any major life threats such as arterial bleeds, I have already ruled out airway obstructions as he has been communicating with me verbally.  My rapid blood sweep reveals bright red blood squirting from the patients left inner thigh.  I pull the makeshift windlass tourniquet from my bag. Even though there was much more advanced versions of this device when I attended SOMC, we were required to make our own out of sticks and handkerchiefs called cravats.  In fact, most of the items in our aid bags at the schoolhouse were hand made.  It taught us resourcefulness.  Plus, if you could get hemorrhage control with one of those antiquated old napkins, achieving it with a fancy CAT2 or ratchet tourniquet would be a breeze!

Tourniquet is in place I call out, "I have homeostasis!"

My instructor pulls on the tourniquet to make sure that it is in place, "You have homeostasis."

There are critical criteria that must be met under specific time limits.  I make the first time cut off for controlling major life threats and move on. The assessment continues with airway, breathing and circulation.  My patient also has a tension pneumothorax, which means that his lung has popped and the air in his plural cavity is keeping it from expanding fully. The immediate treatment involves taking a massive needle and placing it between the ribs just below the collarbone to release the tension. After the primary assessment I will be required to package and transport the patient to our makeshift Combat Support Hospital or CSH (pronounced "cash").  The long-term treatment is to place a chest tube, also known as Tube thoracotomy if you are trying to impress a girl at a bar by convincing her that you're a doctor. This requires that you place a tube the diameter of your thumb between the 5th and 6th rib directly under the armpit.  Since no one I've ever met would ever volunteer for this procedure we were required to verbally walk the instructor through each point.

Everyone that has made it to this point in the course was just required to perform this procedure during the live tissue labs for real so our proficiency had already been displayed. Placement of the Foley catheter was another procedure that we got to talk through, thank God! (Although, we did have to start the procedure using our buddy's actual penis.) Cleaning the site with iodine and preparing for the placement of that huge plastic tube. Right before insertion, we were allowed to trade out for what we called "The Stunt Cock!" Most guys made there own out of a container that we would commonly use to place used needles in called a sharps shuttle. Nothing too fancy, just a container to put the Foley tube in. One of the guys who was transferring from Ranger Battalion to Special Forces had put a significant amount of time into his though. I mean this thing was massive! It was the size of a bottle of Jameson at least, complete with huge nut sack. He even used IV tubing to make it appear veiny. You couldn't help but laugh when he pulled that massive fake dick out. It created levity that was very welcome in the middle of a stressful test.

One of the final procedures that we were required to perform was referred to as the Digital Rectal Exam or DRE. Yep, we had to put our finger into our buddy's ass and check for bleeding. Like all of the other procedures that were being tested on this day we had performed them in a non-testing environment.  We were all aware that this was something that we were going to have to do from the first day and no one was looking forward to it, well maybe a couple of the Navy guys were.  The first time was about a month before, I partnered with another Ranger named Jake because he was skinny and had little fingers. It was a sober day in the schoolhouse, as I would imagine most of the guys had never had a finger in their ass before.  I say most because well, like I said before, the school had several Seals in attendance. Half of the class stood in a row, shoulder to shoulder and was made to drop their BDU bottoms. We looked straight forward as to not make eye contact with the men to our left and right. The goal of the person performing the procedure was to palpate, or feel, the prostate.  Well let's just say that Jake sucks at finding prostates.  His skinny little finger was in my ass for what felt like the first half of a Monday morning after a weekend bender.  After I notice that everyone else is finished and he is still searching, I yell out, "Are you fucking kidding me right now?  Hurry the fuck up!!"  Jake just laughed.  I would get my revenge when it was time to place nasogastric tube but for right now all I could do was curl up in the fetal position and cry.

It came time during our trauma lane assessment for me to check my buddy for intestinal bleeding.  Remembering the psychological trauma that I sustained from Jake the finger twirler, I decided to fake it.  We were told beforehand that if anyone was caught faking this procedure they would have to demonstrate proficiency on themselves in front of the rest of the class, so I was taking a pretty big risk in not going three knuckles deep. I told my partner before hand that if he wanted to avoid the mild molestation then he will grit his teeth and act like a man that has been penetrated when the time comes. Success. The instructor didn't notice. It was the last skill on my assessment. My instructor just shakes his head. My heart sinks into my stomach. What did I forget? He signals me over to meet him outside of the CSH.

"So Ranger, what went wrong?" he asks.

"Nothing Sergeant, I thought that I did everything that I was supposed to."

"Oh so you think your shit was perfect huh? 300 out of 300? You are so fucking shit hot that you didn't miss one single thing? Is that what you think Ranger?"

Now not only did I fail the most important test of this course my teacher thinks that I am an arrogant prick." I take in a deep breath and brace for impact.

"Well," he says, "You'd be right. A perfect 300."

Holy mother fucking shit! I almost don't believe him. This was the biggest hurdle they throw at you in this course and I just passed it! It was like a 2 ton stone was just lifted off of my shoulders. I grew six inches that day. We would still have to make it through a month long clinical rotation and a handful of other tests including the National Registry test for Paramedic but as far as I was concerned I had just made it over the highest mountain in this course.

About a week after Jake accosted me during the DRE we were being tested on nasogastric tube. An NG tube is a long, skinny tube that is inserted into the stomach via the nose. We were instructed not to consume any food prior to practicing this procedure because it is known to create a significant gag response. Knowing that Jake was once again going to be my partner I decided that it was time for reprisal. I ate a half a dozen scrambled eggs with salsa, a huge glass of milk and some yogurt right before we went. We were sitting up in a chair while our partners fed the three foot long tube down our noses, As the gagging begins I become overjoyed. Jake got to wear the smell of my untimely snack for the rest of the morning.

The most anticipated part of the course is the trauma rotations. We are integrated into a hospital and ambulance setting where we are able to apply all of the skills that we have learned over the previous five months. At the time there were three different locations for students to go. I was sent to Bayfront Hospital in Tampa, Florida. We traveled by bus and arrived in the middle of the night. We were set to report to the hospital first thing the next morning but as one keen observer noticed, it was only midnight and there was a bar right next to our condos. Whiskey Joe's would take a substantial amount of my pay that month.

       We hadn't even set our bags down on that first morning when a call came through saying that there was a gunshot victim en route. We were going to be working in three man teams under the direction of the Medical Doctor on duty. Holy shit! The three of us are about to work an actual gunshot wound! One of us would be responsible for establishing an airway, the other an additional IV line and I ended up with "any other" procedures. When the patient rolled in I was slightly confused. It wasn't a fit, early 20's male. For months now we had only worked on each other and for all intents and purposes we all had pretty much the same anatomical landmarks. This was an extremely obese female. She was bleeding from her abdomen and her clothes had already been cut away by the civilian paramedics.

       The two Marine Recon Corpsman that were in charge of airway and circulation jumped right in. I was always impressed with how they handled a situation, a true credit to their unit. Marine Recon Corpsman don't seem to get a lot of credit in the special operations community but I believe that they are some of the most squared away guys that I have ever worked with. I, on the other hand, was at a bit of a loss as to what my role was supposed to be. The nurse informed me that the patient was going to need a Foley catheter. I'm sure that the look on my face was priceless. This wasn't a stunt cock. In fact, the anatomy was completely different than what I had trained for. There was copious amounts of blood and more flaps and folds of fat than I was accustomed to seeing. I was instructed to "get in there." Go on asshole ... lead the way, I thought to myself. I must have spent five minutes trying to get that fucking tube in place. Thankfully the nurse jumped in and saved me. She said some smart ass comment along the lines of, "Don't worry soldier, it happens to lots of guys their first time." It was going to be a long month.

I recall another gentlemen coming into the emergency room whose throat had been diced like a pizza. Apparently he got in an argument with his neighbor who pulled a box cutter on him and used it without hesitation. When he came in his trachea and carotid artery were completely exposed but undamaged. His sternocleidomastoid (muscle of the neck) was severed and had rolled up under the man's jaw. Myself and another medic put over 100 stitches in his neck and chest. Miraculously the man was awake and talking to us the entire time. It was a true testament to how resilient the human body is.

I couldn't help but think back to this patient years later in another special operations medical course that I was attending in Tacoma, Washington. We were conducting a hypervolemia lab. The goal was to simulate the physiological event of losing a majority of the blood in your body. In order to mimic blood loss without actually losing any blood, test subjects (me) took a drug called Lasix, also known as the water pill.  This drug encourages urination.  We then put on a pair of pants that, when inflated, pushed all of the blood to our upper body.  We also took a significant amount of a vasodilator under the tongue to open all of the blood vessels.  We were instructed to stand up as the pants were deflated.  Since all of the blood vessels were wide open, the limited volume of fluid in our system dropped away from the organs and into the legs.  When they checked my blood pressure it was almost undetectable.

We had successfully simulated the loss of about half of the blood in my body.  The doctor asked a series of questions including my name, rank and social security number.  I answered them without hesitation.  He had me complete a couple of squats, again, no issues whatsoever.  The good Doctor then delivered the moral of the story.  An incredibly fit Ranger or Seal in his early 20's is going to compensate right up until the point where he dies.  You can have a guy that has been shot, lost half of the blood in his body and he will still be ready to fight.  As a special operations medic this is something that must always be kept in mind.  The body's resilience in the face of adversity is absolutely astounding.  The amount of abuse that it is able to take and continue functioning is nothing short of miraculous.

Brian was one of the Marine Recon medics on that clinical rotation.  He was a smart guy and had been in the Navy for several years before attending the SOMC. He joked with the man as we put well over 100 stitches in his neck and chest. The two-man job took close to two hours to complete. When the man asked how he looked Brian just replied, "You aren't going to be winning any beauty pageants but you're still alive."

Through the course of my time at the hospital in Florida I was fortunate enough to have scrubbed in on a half a dozen trauma surgeries, assisting the surgeon in the operating room. I helped deliver four babies, one by cesarean section. I placed limbs in casts and stitched up every part of the human body that you can imagine. I did central lines and intubations, worked on people having heart attacks and drunken homeless people that had been stabbed. It wasn't all work though, I would also estimate that my roommate Brian and I both drank our weight in Jameson and managed to find ourselves in the presence of a couple of college aged females once or twice. This was not an easy thing, however, because we were given only two vehicles for a dozen of us. Lack of transportation or time off wouldn't hinder our efforts, however.

We only had a couple of nights off the entire month and the first one that we got I wanted very badly to post up at a dive bar and see if I could break my previous PBR record of 24 in a single evening. Jake, one of my homies in the Special Forces pipeline, had a different plan though. He was friendly with a very attractive girl whose name

I never bothered to learn.  Now Jake put himself in a tough spot because he had the keys to the van that six of us shared but he had told ol' girl that they would be going out on a date.  I don't believe that he explained to her that a squad of very sophomoric special operations guys would be joining them.

I don't remember the name of the nice restaurant that I was dragged into but I do recall not being willing to spend six bucks for a beer.  I also remember trying to set the tablecloth on fire in protest.  Now you might think that is terrible behavior but I was led to this place under the guise that we would be slumming it.  Upon leaving the restaurant I noticed a dive bar across the street with a glorious Pabst Blue Ribbon neon sign illuminated like a beacon that guides a lost sailor home.  Lucky for me I was not the only one in the group that was in need of some good old fashion bar stool therapy.  We had all been elbows deep in blood and guts and could use a flick of the pressure release valve.

I almost threw the barstool when the bartender told me that they didn't stock PBR.  The sign was clearly advertising a certain product.  I asked the bearded gent what the shittiest beer he had was.  He produced from behind the bar a can of Schlitz malt liquor and a small paper bag.  With the grace and fluidity of a symphony conductor he placed the can in the small paper bag and handed it to me.  I could feel the tears welling up as my lip quivered slightly.  I was so happy. So very, very happy.  Ten years later, that very same paper bag is still folded neatly in my wallet to this day.  Every time that I have had a Schlitz since that day I have pulled out that bag and used it like the ghetto koozie that it is.

　　　After consuming enough malt liquor to float a ship it was time to "break the seal." During the course of SOMC I learned that the need to pee more frequently is a hormone reaction.  Alcohol inhibits the production and secretion of antidiuretic hormone (ADH) , which causes more frequent urination.  To this day I have no clue what motivated my next action.  I grabbed a fist full of brown paper towels in the men's room and removed the splashguard from the urinal that I was about to take a piss in.  I said this previously but do not even try to comprehend the cognitive process of a 21-year-old Ranger private with nearly two dozen drinks on board.  I placed the wad of towels containing the rubber treasure deep into my cargo pocket and returned to my barstool.

　　　Earlier in the week I had met a girl who had given me her number.  She had the bad timing of calling me at this very moment.  She said that she was going to be at a bar with a couple of friends and that we should all meet up.  Needless to say this was not a hard sell for the group I was with.

　　　When we arrived we grabbed another drink and met the girls at their table.  I'm sure at this point I was swaying in my seat.  Just as I have no idea why I decided to grab that nasty splashguard out of the urinal, I have no clue why I thought it would be a good idea to retrieve the wad of brown paper towels from my pocket at this moment. I handed them to the girl that invited us and said, "here…. I got you something." Brian was out with us that night and took an interest in the exchange, watching intently as she unwrapped the mystery gift. I could tell that she was not expecting a gift so she was rather excited by the surprise. When all of the paper had been removed she held the diamond shaped red piece of rubber in her bare hands with a perplexed look. Brian's eyes got huge as he realized what it was. It was that look that you would expect a bystander to give if you just kicked a baby for no reason. He tried to control his laughter but the fact that she still had no clue what she was holding was too much for him. He erupted in laughter, tears filling his eyes. Now she was really confused. I leaned over to her and said, "Any asshole could bring you flower, how's that for original?"

"Jesus Christ, Jenkins!" replied another buddy once he realized what was going on. He told her what she was holding was what kept piss from splashing back on your hands at the urinal. To everyone's surprise she started laughing. She looked at me and said, "That's funny, disgusting but funny."

Interestingly one of the girls that met up with us that night and one of my buddies ended up getting married a couple of years later. It is also my understanding that she kept my special gift for several years.

A year and a half later I would have the privilege of attending another similar rotation in Atlanta, Georgia at Grady Hospital. There is no other training in the world that can compare to it. It is the most comprehensive, progressive program for medics on earth. Following this training I felt prepared to handle any injury that I saw on the field of battle. Which was a good thing because within two weeks of graduating SOMC I would be deployed to Afghanistan to act as a platoon medic for Charlie Company, 3rd Ranger Battalion.

Drinking from a firehouse! These were the books assigned to us on the first day of SOMC.

Extreme log PT at the schoolhouse. 6-mile stroll through Ft. Bragg with over 100lbs to carry, before class starts.

Staying proficient at Ranger skills. We jumped several times while at SOMC.

SOMC graduation.  Chris and I being cheery as fuck!

SOMC Graduation.  Sitting with some of my Navy
friends.  That's Lewis Lewis behind me.

.....

## Chapter 6 - Time Consumer

I had been a soldier in the United States Army for the past 18 months.  Most guys that I went to basic training with had already deployed to Iraq or Afghanistan.  I had spent the last year and a half in various schools preparing to be a member of special operations.  Every hurdle that was bounded gave me an increasing level of confidence in my ability to operate among the world's best soldiers.  All of that confidence was stripped away when I took my fist step off of the back of that Air Force cargo plane onto the runway on Bagram Airfield.  The mountains that surrounded the airfield did well to show me how insignificant I was.  I had done some hiking growing up in Arizona but my perspective on what a mountain was changed instantly as my size 10.5 combat boot hit the tarmac. As my eyes opened wide in awe, I could feel the brisk sting of the cold dry air and took in a lung full of air like I've never smelled before.  It was different, almost ancient.  In all my travels since that day I have never smelled that same smell again except for the two other times I would step off of a plane in Afghanistan.

I suddenly realized that in all that we were taught we never really learned exactly what we would be doing.  I almost expected to start taking rocket fire the moment that I stepped off the plane. I knew about the Ranger mission from stories and movies but I really didn't understand what my role was supposed to be yet.  Furthermore I didn't know a single person who I would be working with. My entire Battalion had deployed a month earlier and I had never met any of them.  I was the FNG (Fucking New Guy).  None of my accomplishments up to this point meant a damn thing.  No one knew me.  I would have to prove myself once again.

On my very first day in country I met up with who I thought would be my platoon.  We had to do some fast rope training.  The act of it was simple enough, grab the rope that was dangling from the back of the helicopter and slide down it like a fire pole.  This was actually the first time I had ever actually been in a helicopter, which didn't help with the anxiety.  On one of the last evolutions one of the squad leaders sprained his ankle pretty badly. I had not expected this to be my first patient as a Ranger medic.  I had prepared for gunshot wounds and bones sticking out and giant stunt cocks.  The majority of the training at the schoolhouse was targeted at the worst possible scenario.  He honestly would have been better off had he been shot.  I froze up a little.  He didn't need me to check his airway or start an IV.  There was no major life threats or hemorrhaging to control.  My aidbag wasn't packed to treat this injury.  I had some pain meds but I didn't have the right size needles to do a simple intramuscular injection. This was more like a sick call injury; this wasn't what I was supposed to see in combat. The Staff Sergeant screamed in pain as I plunged an 18-gauge needle into his shoulder.

"Fuck Doc! I feel like I just got arm raped! Do you even know what the fuck you are doing?"

I wanted to tell him how good I did on my trauma lane in SOMC but none of that shit matters here. I'm fucking this up bad. I wrap his ankle the way that you would expect a monkey to if you threw a splint and a couple of bananas in his cage. I was a fucking soup sandwich. The only thing that saved me in the long run was I ended up getting attached to a different platoon and forward deployed the next day to another outpost. If I had to work as that man's medic for the next three months I'm pretty sure that I would have been fucked.

I arrived at what would be my home for the next few months. I recall standing in a formation with a dozen or so guys. The process of deciding which guys would go to each platoon was not quite what I had imagined it would be. The platoon Sergeants stood in front of the wide-eyed new Rangers and began a selection process that I can only compare to a game of kickball in grade school. There was no inquiry or interview at all. "He looks strong, I'll take him." Really? Like cattle at a livestock auction. I was beginning to get incredibly self-conscious about not getting picked in the first three rounds when I realized that all of the non-infantry guys had been put in the back row for a reason. Our fate had already been decided. We would become the property of our section leaders. Mine was a six-foot tall gentleman with a shaved head and a full leg piece tattoo. Awesome, another Runza. In the deepest voice that you could possibly imagine he yelled my name.

"JENKINS over here!"

This guy was going to be whom I reported to from here out and he looked like the poster child for the Aryan race. Dano, as he was known as to everyone that wasn't a cherry fuck, was the epitome of what I had always imagined a Ranger to be. His demeanor was beyond intimidating.

There is a very real learning curve to being a Ranger. I had 18 months of training but no real perspective as to what day-to-day life looked like. Minutes after meeting my new senior medic I learned that what it looked like was four cots in the back of a tent that also served as the medical facility to two platoons of injury prone guys thousands of miles from their moms. I was shown which one of the "bunks" was mine, dropped the single bag that I would be living out of for the next few months and given a short tour of the base. I believe that the other new Rangers that I came over with were not having such an easy introduction into the Regiment but most of them had only been in the Army about five months. The look on some of their faces at the chow hall later that first day resembled the look a dog has right after it has been kicked for shitting in the house.

My first week seemed to be a series of tests. My senior medic quizzed me randomly on drug protocols and assessment techniques.  He took me out on a couple of death runs in hopes that I would fall off of his pace.  The fact that I had been obsessed with physical fitness before this and spent at least a couple of hours a day training truly paid off.  By showing that I was fit to fight on my first few days I showed that I was responsible and partially trustworthy.  The military works differently than the rest of the world.  I have always said that success really only relies on three things: be in good shape, always be early for everything and always have a clean well-groomed appearance.  It wasn't long before I fucked one of those three things up.

A few weeks into my first deployment and I was coasting.  I had done some cool guy CQB (Close Quarter Battle) training with my platoon. I went out to the range and shot every piece of weaponry a kid could dream about.  I rode in helicopters and even did a couple of missions.  I was finally a real Ranger. I was watching a movie on a shitty 13-inch TV in my tent when a young private ran in.  Out of breath he told me frantically that Dano was looking for me and that I was late for a training meeting.  Training meeting?  No one told me about a....

"Doc, come on!"

When I arrived at the headquarters tent everyone seemed to be on a bit of a study break. My boss looked at me like he was trying to melt my face with his eyes. He was fucking pissed. The First Sergeant told everyone to take their seats. Apparently we were half way through a two-hour PowerPoint presentation that I was unaware of. You see, the military has a very deliberate chain of command. The First Sergeant tells his platoon sergeants something, they tell their squad leaders, the squad leaders pass it on to their team leaders, the team leaders scream it at their privates while making them do push ups. It's highly effective except no one ever thinks to tell the medic what the fuck is going on. I hadn't blown this training off; I simply didn't know it was happening. That didn't matter. When the training ended everyone else left the tent to go on with their day. Myself and the other platoon medic, who was also unaware of the training, got to stay back for some "extra training."

We tried to explain that no one had told us what was going on while we were sweating buckets in the front leaning rest position. Our senior medic said something that was very simple yet has stuck with me to this day.

"This is your company. It is your responsibility to know what is going on without someone telling you. You have to be proactive not reactive or you will not survive here." It was one of the most valuable lessons of my first combat deployment.

Another highly valuable lesson that I learned was that, under no circumstance, should you ever let someone know that it's your birthday.  One of the privates in my platoon made this mistake and paid for it dearly.  He found himself drenched in water and shaving cream, zip tied to a chain link fence for two hours in the middle of the night in the middle of December.  As tough as he was, he was no match for the six Rangers dressed in all black with night vision goggles waiting to ambush him on his way back from the porta shitter.  A cold, lonely, miserable birthday present that would likely get the gifters demoted or worse today.

To be honest, that first deployment was not what I was expecting from a combat standpoint.  There was a few missions, one or two guys got shot but for the most part it was more about finding a way to spend our days without going crazy than it was about finding and eradicating the enemy.  I remember watching all three Godfather movies in a single day while eating six whole boxes of thin mint Girl Scout cookies that someone's mom had sent.  I went to the gym at least twice a day and jerked off in porta potty.  Not the high-speed life that I had expected.  By the end of that deployment I was deadlifting over 600 pounds and still running a sub 13-minute two mile.

When it was time to come home I envisioned the scene that I had watched time and time again on television where a group of service members land on some runway and were greeted with crowds of loved ones waving flags and welcome home signs. That didn't happen. Not even close. We landed on a military base in the middle of the night, walked into a hangar where three medics were giving guys shots, took a short bus ride to our company area where guys turned in their weapons and went home. It was the most unceremonious thing imaginable.

For a few of us it was our first time coming home but many of these men were already on their fourth or fifth deployment. Several of them made the initial jump into Afghanistan. My company was the same one that executed Operation Rhino on October 19th, 2001. By 2004 they were already battle-hardened men and I had a lot of catching up to do. Sure, I now had a combat scroll and a CMB (Combat Medic Badge), but I still didn't have my trial by fire. I still didn't feel like a real Ranger.

The aid station in Salarneo forward operating base.

Aziz,  the

local bread maker and me.

Cool Guy training. Salerno forward operating base

.....

## Chapter 7 - Welcome Home

Coming home from war was a very surreal experience. Citizens have a preconceived notion as to what goes on "over there." Sadly, however, these notions are often based solely on the latest Hollywood blockbuster that they shelled out nine bucks to see. People treat you in accordance with their inaccurate beliefs as to what occurs during war. At this time, everyone in the country still conveyed a great deal of support for our efforts overseas. Everyone back home seemed so proud of me yet I didn't feel like I had done anything. Sure there had been a couple of small exchanges but I was expecting Black Hawk Down level action and to be honest, I think that is what the majority of people that knew me thought that I had gone through. Friends spoke to me differently and men that I looked up to growing up in the fire station gave me a great deal of respect. I felt honored by the experience but I also felt like a bit of a liar. I was no war hero I was just happy to be home.

While home on leave I told my dad that I needed him to teach me how to drive a motorcycle. He had just purchased a brand new Harley Road King and still had his older Honda. He seemed to be having a blast watching me struggle with the clutch in a parking lot near our house. We spent a couple of quality hours laughing at my lack of coordination. There was so many things that I had never done, so many places that I hadn't been.  Returning from deployment opened my eyes to that.  I wanted to experience all of life. I wanted to see it all, touch it, smell it, and embrace all of what life has to offer. When we got home I told my dad, "We should go to Vegas!"

"What?"

"Yeah Dad, you and me should take the motorcycles to Vegas after your next shift!"

"You don't know how to ride a motorcycle."

"The fuck I don't, you just taught me."

I knew that Bruce wasn't in a position to turn down such a request from his son, the war hero.  I had never been to Vegas and I wanted to check that box in an epic way.  When Jess and I were freezing our stones off during RIP we started talking about all the places that we had been.  I said that I had drunk a beer in 7 different states, a fact that I was proud of at the time.  I made a short list and decided that I wanted to take a run at the entire country.  I set a goal to drink a beer in every state in my four-year enlistment. Nevada was next on my list.

My pops agreed that as long as I got my permit while he was at work the following day we would go when he got home.  Of course I stayed out until 4am catching up with my friends the night before we were going to go.  It didn't matter.  I was packing the saddlebags at 8:30 when he arrived home from the fire station.  He asked me what I was doing as if we hadn't talked about a seven-hour motorcycle ride to sin city.

"Well," I informed him, "We are fucking going to Vegas!"  I pulled out my permit and shot him a crooked grin.  I don't think that my dad has ever really been surprised by any of the shit that I have pulled but he had a look on his face that morning for sure.  Obviously my dad is a champ.  He went and put on a pair of blue jeans, had a cup of coffee and called my stepmom to let her know he would be in Vegas for the next three days.  They had waited until I returned home to have their wedding so they had been married for less than a week and he was taking off with me to hit the strip.  The man is hands down the best dad on the fucking planet.

As we accelerated to over 60 mph I began to regret my decision.  I had never been out of a parking lot on two wheels.  Here we were on a desert highway with 18-wheelers buzzing past us.  I've never clenched onto anything as hard as I death gripped those handle bars but we made it.  We made it every bit of those 275 miles without a single stall; I didn't dump that thing once and when we arrived, the ear-to-ear grin on my dad's face made the terrifying journey 100% worth it.  It was that moment that I think most dads wait for, the time when your son also gets to be your best friend, when you get to do cool shit with him not just be his parent.

He taught me how to play poker and wouldn't you know it I pulled off a royal flush. I was playing a buck a hand but the jackpot was still over $1,400. I was unaware of the rule but my father informed me that if you hit a hand like that you are obligated to pay for drinks for the rest of the trip. I was happy to oblige after all that he had done for me. It was three of the most fun days that I can remember, sans the hung-over ride back through the desert.

Before I knew it my 2 weeks of leave was up and it was time to head back to Battalion. This would be my first full training cycle where I would finally learn all of the cool trade secrets on how to kill a dozen men with my bare hands and shoot laser beams from my eyes.

......

## Chapter 8 - Away We Go

In all honesty there is nothing really glamorous about the day-to-day life of a Ranger medic.  The alarm clock snaps you awake at 4:45 in your dorm style barracks room that you share with another guy.  Five minutes to hit the three S's (Shit, shower, shave) and out the door.  After a short walk you open the aid station and wait for the guys to start coming in.  On any given day we would have 3-6 guys come in with a mild complaint, usually something that happened during training or something that he contracted from playing with the ladies in downtown Columbus.  If a guy has a medical issue that is outside of our scope of practice we would take him across the street to the Battalion Aid Station (BAS).  The BAS had a handful of medics, a Physician's Assistant and a surgeon.  It had a fully stocked pharmacy and multiple treatment rooms.  There really isn't too much that we couldn't treat in house.

Shortly after sick call the entire company would do PT.  Most of the time I was trusted to do my own thing but every once in awhile someone would do something stupid at a bar and we would all get punished for it.  After PT we would eat breakfast and get ready for whatever training was on the plate for the day.  We drilled all the time.  Airborne operations, demo practice, rifle time, medical training and then some.  A 15-hour day was not at all uncommon. We trained and trained and trained. Between the constant deployments and this type of a day-to-day grind when we were in the states I have no clue how guys stayed married. I have so much respect for Ranger families; they get put through the grind right along with us. I don't know how some of the guys managed to have a wife and kids through all of that.

CQB training on Ft. Benning, Georgia.

By the end of that first training cycle I had things pretty well figured out.  I moved out of the barracks and in with my friend Matt.  Matt was in charge of the medics that had graduated RIP but were waiting to go to SOMC and had already gone to Ranger school and deployed once with Regiment.  The scar on the back of his head was still very visible from our Panama City outing a year and a half earlier.

"Should we have a BBQ for the fourth of July this weekend?"  Asked Matt.

"This is America isn't it?" I respond.

It is the final days of June 2005 and I was already preparing to leave on my second combat deployment.  Matt and I shared a two story, three-bedroom condo that was considered "on-post" housing on Fort Benning.  Just as Matt and I begin planning our 'Happy Birthday America' debauchery, I received a page from my company to return immediately.  This means one of two things.  One, some moron got caught doing something illegal so our entire company has to come in and pee in a little plastic cup or we are getting a high profile mission which will require us to be wheels up in the next 18 hours.

As always, deployment bags are already packed and staged in the zoo. The zoo was what we called our company headquarters.  It was a dismal building void of windows or fresh air.  It was divided into separate platoon areas by giant wall lockers.  There was a communications shop, supply and the aid station that I spent years pretending to be productive in.

Most of the guys live within the brown barbwire fence of our compound, so by the time I arrive there is already a shit storm of chaos. Rangers were running around frantically looking for various pieces of mission essential equipment and speculating as to what was going on. I knew better than to ask my platoon Sergeant what was happening.

I was very recently transferred to 1st platoon. They had just undergone a command change and a man I will call SFC Bent had recently taken over as platoon sergeant. He was one of the cadres responsible for torturing me during RIP. His cruelty rivaled that of SSG Runza so I had plenty of reasons to keep my distance. At this point I didn't really care what was going on as long as I didn't have to pee in that fucking cup!

By nightfall we were boarding a cargo plane on what felt like an abandoned runway on Ft. Benning and I still didn't know what was going on. Popular is the guy with a cargo pocket full of Ambien on an 18-hour flight in a noisy military flight. I passed that shit out like Skittles on Halloween. Those flights are very uncomfortable for several reasons. First of all the seats are just cargo nets, we are allowed to lay on the metal floor once the plane hits a certain altitude but laying on cold steel for the better part of a day isn't exactly luxurious. Most guys opt out by taking the popular sleeping pill and going black for several hours. The next thing I remember is landing in Germany to refuel, still groggy from the double dose of that happy little white pill.

The second leg of the flight would be far less restful as I begin to get information on what we are doing. Apparently there was a group of Navy Seals that were compromised in some remote province of Afghanistan and we were going in to act as a Combat Search and Rescue team (CSAR). I know what you are thinking; I thought the exact same thing. Why wouldn't they deploy a team that was already in Afghanistan? Well, they did. This became the next point of my great unrest. An MH-47 "Chinook" helicopter containing eight members of the 160th Special Operations Aviation Regiment (SOAR) and eight U.S. Navy Seals was shot down en route to aid the compromised members of Seal Team 10 as a Quick Reaction Force (QRF). All of those men lost their lives in an effort to come to the aid of their brothers.

Upon landing at Bagram Air Field (BAF) our platoon has just enough time to grab ammo and MRE's and meet at the airfield. My stomach sinks as I find out that our Chinook will be following the identical flight path of the one that was recently shot down. We sit on the airfield waiting for darkness to fall over the distant mountains that will soon become the proving ground for our young platoon. While we wait we see a group of A10 pilots getting ready to take off. As if they knew exactly where we were about to go they give us a strong thumbs up from the cockpit. Members from each of the different branches of the military love to give each other a hard time, but when it comes down to it there is a very deep level of respect for the job that others do. We didn't realize it at the time but these men would be our salvation once we hit the ground. It was evident by the gesture that they gave us from their cockpit that they had a great deal of respect for the job that we were about to do.

"The stars will cry the blackest tears tonight, and this is the moment that I live for...And I'm here to sing the anthem of our dying day." The lyrics speak directly to me from the mp3 player stashed in my shoulder pocket. The popping of the snare drum matches the rhythm of the cover fire being laid down by the flight crew. It's dark as we exit the back of the hovering Chinook. I can make out the outline of each one of the other Rangers that have, without order, formed a semi-circle formation. We face out and pull security as the bird pulls away into the night. And in an instant we sit in silence. The stars are in abundance like I have never before seen. Even surrounded by a platoon of Rangers, I feel entirely alone. Stranded in the middle of nowhere. The air is cold and thin. One at a time we pick up and move to a rally point and I can already feel the effects of the high altitude stealing my breath.

To my surprise we see a group of guys sitting around a campfire.  They looked like a small contingent of Special Forces guys but they could have been Seals.  I didn't ask.  I was just amazed that they had built a campfire!  It didn't seem like the most operationally sound decision to me but then again what did I know.

Even as we set up a patrol base I am still not entirely sure what is going on.  Not surprising considering that I spent most of my first year as a Ranger having almost no clue as to what was actually happening.  At a company level the first sergeant delegates to his platoon sergeants, those platoon sergeants pass the information to their squad leaders, the squad leaders pass the info to their team leaders who pass it to their privates.  You may not have picked up on it but "let the medic know what the fuck is going on" isn't really in that chain.  Most of the time I had to pester one of my buddies who was a team leader to let me know what we were doing.

One of the guys begins to complain of a severe headache and I am worried that it may be altitude sickness.  48 hours ago we were sitting at sea level and if I was cool enough to have one of those sweet GPS watches like the other guys I could tell you that we were sitting at nearly 10,000ft.  Even if someone did get altitude sickness there wasn't much I could do about it.  The treatment calls for a drug called Mannitol, in a dose that would have been way too much to carry with me. It was a risk that we were going to be taking.

The first night is quiet but no one sleeps. The entire platoon understands that this is a very important mission. As the sun rises it exposes the most beautiful country that my eyes have ever seen. It was the most expansive, remote and wild terrain imaginable. Even at the end of June when the midday highs would reach 100+ there were snow-capped mountains in the distance.

My gazing session would be short lived, the sun was up and it was time to begin our first patrol. My inexperience is made evident as I realize that having both an aid bag and an assault pack would make navigating this terrain miserable. Why did I bring two bags? I use a carabineer to snap the two together. Within the first 40 meters of our movement I realized this was going to be awful! The assault pack is sitting on top of my aid bag and every step causes it to swing around to the side and smack me in the head. If you're going to be dumb you better be tough I suppose and I was stupid for not packing more effectively.

We traverse some of the gnarliest terrain my feet have ever experienced. We have shifted from a wedge type formation into a more snake like single file. I am the third to last person in the movement. The guy behind me is an Air Force Combat Controller. The guy behind him is an Afghan Special forces member known as a "Mohawk" that was on loan from our OGA (Other

Governmental Agency) buddies.  I ask them both if they get the feeling that we are being followed.  They both have the same feeling.  I hear footsteps behind us.  We're being hunted.  Maybe not the same way Apollo Creed and Governor Schwarzenegger were hunted in that Predator movie, but it was still pretty eerie.  I relayed this information to my Platoon Sergeant that was directly ahead of me.  This was my first mission as SFC Bent's medic as he was recently assigned to 3rd Battalion.  He took over our platoon several weeks before this deployment and I had attempted to avoid him as best as I could in the train up.  I would come to find out later that he was a great guy but at this time all that I remember of him was him making me low crawl through a partially frozen mud puddle in December at Cole Range during RIP.

Not more than thirty seconds after I relay the information to him I hear POP POP POP POP.

"Enemy target, 200 meters to the right!" one of the squad leaders announces.

Every weapon system in the platoon orients in that direction.  As my Platoon Sergeant spins to get eyes on the target he loses his footing.  He slides 30 feet down the steep terrain and is finally stopped by a stump.  My first thought was, that's what you get for making me crawl in that fucking ice pond you prick!  That thought was quickly followed by the instinct to run in the direction of the enemy.  I took off, in a hard sprint up that hill and to the right of our platoon.  I dropped behind a cluster of rocks that provided a perfect cover for the firefight that was sure to take place. My Platoon Sergeant makes his way up the mountainside and settles in next to my location. I ask him if he is alright but I really didn't really care. My focus was on the fact that I was about to be in a real deal Taliban versus Ranger firefight and I was ready.

Nothing. Nothing happened. A few quick shots from one our guys and then nothing. It was like having a random girl at a bar grab your junk then just leave. Now here I am left with a combat chub and nothing to shoot at. Within a few minutes we pick up and continued our movement, at times having to literally crawl on our hands and knees in certain areas.

My good friend Josh, who has the very appropriate nickname "the angry leprechaun" has the unfortunate task of hauling the ammo for the 240B. A 240B is a belt fed weapon that dispenses 7.62 rounds like confetti at a parade. Josh was a stud for sure; he wrestled in college and had that 'I'd rather die than give up' attitude, which is a common theme among successful Rangers. The combination of the altitude, heat and 60+ pounds of gear will wear on anyone, however, and he was no exception. I can tell that he is getting his lunch money taken and ask him if he wants an IV. He refuses so I give him some Gatorade and sit with him for a moment. He recovers and we continue to crawl up the side of that steep mountain. This makes me much more aware of how the men are responding to these rigors. I felt okay but I spent a decent amount of time in my youth hunting in the mountains of Northern Arizona. My father and I would cover 30+ miles in a weekend hunt across some demanding terrain. And while this made that feel like walking from Cinnabon down to the Hot Topic at the Arrowhead Mall, it was still a better indoctrination than my friend from Iowa would have ever had.

As the sun sets on our first day in the Kunar we set up a patrol base. Do you remember that kid in school that asked, "when are we ever going to use this? Why do we have to learn this?"

Well, that kid was me in basic training when we were going over how to set up a claymore mine. A claymore is a directional, anti-personnel mine that saw heavy use in Vietnam but has become a relic of sorts by modern warfare standards. Right up there with the bayonet. So needless to say, when my Platoon Sergeant gave the order for us to set them up just outside of the patrol base I nearly shit myself. I mean seriously, it's 2005 and we are Rangers! Don't we have something a little more high speed than a fucking claymore?! Luckily for me, the instructions "Front toward enemy" were idiot proof. (Sorry Matt, I know that's why you got No-Go'ed in Ranger school.)

With our cool guy booby traps in place and the first watch posted up I decided to check on each of the guys. I walk around checking feet for blisters, handing out pieces of candy from my 'morale pouch' and making sure that no one had sustained any injuries throughout the day. Some time during the night we get a care package in the form of a 1-ton pallet dropped from a C-130 cargo plane, full of water, medical supplies, food and batteries. I gather up several IV bags and pre-package them with everything necessary to get a line started. I make four of these and give one to each of the squad leaders. One of them complains about having to carry the weight. I explain to him that I already have six of them in my bag, plus every bit of equipment that he is carrying. The next morning I find the blue package hidden in the bush where he was laying the night before. What a shit head. I pick up the bag and add it to the contents of my pack.

My Platoon Sergeant calls me over and says that we need to set up a choke point. I'm at a complete loss. I have no idea what he was talking about. I thought it might be some other Vietnam area Ranger trap. I felt pretty dumb when he just wanted me to take a knee and count the Rangers walking out of the patrol base to make sure that we had everyone.

It's midday and we have been walking for hours. The temperature on my buddies cool guy watch says 102. We find the set of huts that we suspect was the home of some of the Taliban members that were involved in the firefight. We find a decent spot to set up over watch and a team goes into the house. It's more of a shack really. It has dirt floors and only 3 walls made of sticks and mud. There is a fireplace and a couple of utensils. There is a section of the hut designated for chickens. This guy definitely wins the award for lowest carbon footprint. I will say this, the view more than made up for his lack of appliances. It was breathtaking. You could see terraces across the ravine and mountains in the distance that were snow covered. No one was there, well besides the chickens. We do a quick search that comes up pretty flat. As we are searching a near by ravine I hear a call come over the radio.

"There's monkeys."

"Repeat last."

"Ummmm, there is a pack of big ass baboons staring at us. And so help me God if they get any closer I am going to open up on them with the 240!"

It was Josh on over watch. Now I know what you're thinking, "There aren't any baboons in Afghanistan." Well listen here: that shit happened! There are a dozen Rangers that will confirm it. It was a pack of huge, fang-toothed baboons!

We keep our distance and patrol the area in small teams looking for any signs of a firefight. One of the patrol teams finds several 5.56 shell casings so we know that this is where shit went down but there was no sign of the Seals.

Four guys with very impressive beards, wearing shorts walk up to our over watch position. They are members of Seal Team 10. My first thought was, look at these shit bags wearing shorts. Then I realized that it's over 100 degrees out and shorts would be pretty awesome!  Wait, why the fuck are we wearing pants?  And long sleeve DCU tops?  Damn I should have gone to BUDs.  We exchange information.  They tell us that they have Intel that one of the local goat herders has information on one of the missing Seals.

We move out to the houses in the valley below.  A couple of our guys accompany the Seals while myself and the other half of our platoon pull security.  They find out that the body of one of the Seal operators was nearby.  One of the locals agrees to show us where for a price.  I'm not sure what they paid the man but I imagine that it was difficult for those guys to not pay that guy with a throat punch.

We recover the body of Matt Axelson, a Navy Seal from California who turned 29 just 3 days prior. They must have anticipated what had happened, one of the Seals pulls out a black body bag. Throughout my time in the military I have been exposed to countless acts of absolute professionalism, this moment ranks among the top. Those four men refuse our help.  They will carry their brother out themselves.  A decision that I hold in the highest regard.

It's just starting to get late and we begin to move away from the shacks.  As we set up another patrol base we call for another resupply drop.  This one doesn't come quite as close as the last one did.

It impacts the side of the mountain with the force of a Mac truck striking a Jetta on the freeway. The palate explodes, which really wouldn't be an issue if it hadn't impacted on a portion of the mountain that featured about a 20% grade slope. This caused a diarrhea like explosion of water bottles and MRE's scattering our supplies all the way down the mountainside. By this point, we were pretty fatigued and definitely dehydrated. The thought of having to climb down that mountain to recover our water was a little heartbreaking. A team is assigned to do the recovery. There are a couple of body bags in the supply drop. We use one of them to carry our food and water back up the mountain to our patrol base. We are able to recover about half a bags worth for our entire platoon. It would have to get spread pretty thin.

Back in the patrol base I begin checking feet and general morale. My platoon Sergeant's feet are wet. I dig into my bag and pull out a small container of foot powder and a fresh pair of socks. He tilts his head a little and says, "Squared away Doc!" It was the first compliment I ever received from him and it did well to raise my spirits.

It was just about to be dark out and I found a perfect little spot under a bush to finally get some sleep. I couldn't have been asleep for more than an hour when I am snapped awake by the sound of an A10 Thunderbolt, "fast mover" dropping hate on targets via some big ass American bombs. It was the same pilots that gave us the thumbs up as we were waiting to board the Chinook.  They were looking out for us, our guardian angels no doubt.  The first explosion was so close!  My eyes shot open, my brain told my hand to reach for my rifle but my body refused to respond.  I was paralyzed with fear. I literally can't move!  My pants are wet.  Did I piss myself?!  As my hyperventilating begins to subside, I am finally able to turn my head.  I look around to see the rest of my platoon in a hyper-vigilant state. I take a knee and give my pants the sniff test.  Its not urine, that's good!  It looks like it started to rain a little while I was asleep.  The bomb runs done by the A10's continued throughout the night.  They call it a show of force.  And if I was that scared, I'm sure those Taliban assholes were shitting themselves.

I wasn't able to sleep after that.  Years later a group of kids threw a firecracker outside of my bedroom window in the middle of the night.  It brought me back to that very moment in time with such reality that I didn't sleep for two nights afterward.

By sun up I had taken three extra guard shifts so that the guys could get a little more sleep. There was no way that I was going to be able to sleep so some of the other guys might as well get a few extra minutes under the covers. Being up all night allowed me the opportunity to see another picturesque sunrise.  It is possible that it seemed so spectacular due to the vast untouched countryside that it sprawled out over but it has been my experience that no sunrise ever looks as good as the one that comes after a night filled with near death experiences.  If I had to guess I would say that the sun rises in a glorious spectrum of color and sanguinity analogous to the birth of a child every morning.  We just see that hope more clearly after it has been nearly taken from us forever.

The morning light means that we are moving again.  My PSG and I set up another choke point to count everyone off.  This time I know what it means, by this point I am becoming a pro at counting to 38.  So far the terrain that we had experienced had been the most austere I have ever traversed and it was about to get even worse.

Within an hour the world just dropped off.  We found ourselves descending down 500 or so meters of loose slate rock that was at an unbelievably steep grade.  I'm still not sure how those men had conducted a firefight in this environment.  The layered rock would frequently break under the weight of the Ranger's feet, sending large sharp rocks tumbling past the men below.  I am honestly shocked that no one was seriously injured during this movement.  In addition to the danger that the falling rocks presented, we were so incredibly exposed.  If the enemy were to set in the right position they would have been able to take out our entire platoon with a single machine gun.

When we reached the bottom of the cliff we came upon the village that we had been searching for.  Chills shoot down my spine as we find shards of

American uniforms on the ground just outside the village.  The bloody pieces of camouflage clothing that so closely resembled the very same ones that I had on served as a startling reminder of how real this situation was.  This wasn't a training exercise.  No one was carrying blanks and no one would be calling index at the end.

We need to speak to the village elder in hopes of gaining some information.  Something seems out of place.  My Platoon Sergeant and I both notice a man that is way too well kept to be a goat herder.  His crisp clean white tunic is in direct contrast to the general appearance of every other member of the village.  His sparkling gold watch was not something that a goat herder would be wearing.  The rest of the villagers are in old tattered garments with dirty snarled hair and beards.  They resemble how I would imagine the characters of the bible.  Trapped in some sort of mountainous time capsule, preserved from the rest of the world for two thousand years.  We keep an eye on the out-of-place man but can't really do anything about it. We are in no position to start slinging accusations.  We are out numbered at least 10 to 1, that we can see and we are trying to play nice.  We are in their village attempting to get information that will hopefully lead to the recovery of our brothers in arms, harassing one of the locals will easily shut down their hospitality so he gets a pass.

We get little from the village elder. The guys that conduct the interview said that he was very apprehensive about giving any information, that he seemed scared. This isn't uncommon in Afghanistan. The vast majority of the population is simple, hard-working farmers and herders. They are bullied and intimidated by a select few whose contorted interpretation of a religious ideology has left them in the crossfire.

As we leave the village we are notified that we are being extracted. We need to move roughly 9 kilometers to our exfil point. Typically, that isn't a distance that would make any one of us break a sweat. However, at this point almost everyone was severely dehydrated and without any water. It was over 100 degrees and this was some of the nastiest country in the world. We would be extracted just past dark so it only gave us a few hours to get to our grid coordinate. Most of the platoon had done well to hide their discomfort up until this point. Those 9 kilometers were the breaking point though. Guys started to really fall apart at this point. Most of us had less than 4 hours of sleep in the past 72 hours, add in the lack of acclimatization to the high altitude and the lack of water and we were getting close to becoming combat ineffective.

I started an IV on the RTO (Radio Telephone Operator). His eyes were rolling to the back of his head and he was tachycardic. His skin was hot and dry. He had literally sweated out everything in his system. His body no longer had the ability to cool itself and his temperature was increasing rapidly. That poor son of a bitch was carrying around that 117F radio this entire time. With the extra batteries that radio added over 20 more pounds to his pack. I started to get concerned for the rest of the men knowing that our RTO is a pretty tough guy. I remember back to the lessons learned at OEMS (Operational Emergency Medical School) about Rangers being able to compensate right up to the point of death. If these guys were displaying these kinds of symptoms it wouldn't be long before we were having to carry some of them out. Placing one guy and all of his equipment into a litter places a massive burden on the rest of the platoon and in this environment is almost guaranteed to create a domino effect. If he is this bad off it's only a matter of time before more guys start going down.

I quickly make my way up to the front of the file formation asking how each guy is along the way. Once I get to the front I stop and face the men as they walk past me. I was attempting to see how well they were focusing, if anyone was stumbling or showing any other signs of distress. The thing about Rangers, and most members of special operations, is they won't always tell you that they are hurt. They pride themselves on their ability to endure incredible amounts of suffering. So I had to be a little tricky and observe them as they walked by. When the very last guy reached me I repeated the process, running back to the front of the formation in an effort to look each man in the eyes. I did this at least three more times before reaching our exfil point.  One of our newer guys who was on his first deployment was sitting, head down when I came upon him.  He was displaying all of the same symptoms as our RTO.

"Hey Brandon, are you alright bud?"

"Yeah Doc, I'm just a little out of breath."

"What's the matter, you're not used to walking for three days at 10,000 feet in hundred degree weather without water?"

"Ha, no Doc, I guess I'm not."

"Well, you look good.  I mean that, you're a good looking man!"

Brandon just smiles and shakes his head.  We need to get moving.  I have a small packet of Gatorade at the bottom of my pack.  I take it out and mix it with the last 8 ounces of hot water that I have left.  *Drink this.*  After another couple of minutes Brandon stands up.  Not the way that a six foot, 200 pound Ranger usually stands, it was more like the way a fawn stands for the first time.  I could see that he didn't have much left in him.  I do the math in my head.  With several more clicks to travel I decide that carrying his 35 pound assault pack would be a lot easier than attempting to drag his 200 pound ass in a skedco.

"Let me see your pack bud."

His squad leader says, "No, I'll take it Doc."

"Roger that Sergeant."

I chuckle as I see the frustration mounting in the squad leaders face as the second pack bobbles and hits him in the side of the head.  He makes some comment about how bad this sucks.

"Yeah, tell me about it Sergeant, my second bag has been hitting me for the last three days." He looks at me with awe as if his pack was the heaviest one on anyone's back this entire time.  He doesn't complain again.

We are getting close now.  The last 2 kilometers are a straight shot.  We're moving uphill on an old dirt road.  I move through the platoon and ask how guys are doing one more time.  Arter projectile vomits but never even slows down; he doesn't miss a single step.  What a tough son of a bitch.  He's been carrying that 240B this whole time.  Without any ammo that belt fed weapon weighs nearly 30 pounds.  I have no idea how he made it up and down some of those rock faces with that massive, cumbersome weapon system.  His squad leader tells Arter to give him the weapon.  Arter refuses, he won't give up his weapon.  Tough, prideful impressive bastard.  He vomits one more time without skipping a beat.  My dehydrated heart swells with pride knowing that I am in the same unit with men like this.  We had all put ourselves through a torturous selection process, not for a special colored hat or arm insignia but for the honor and privilege of working along side me like that; men who, in the most inhospitable environment, under the greatest stress imaginable, refuse to back down an inch.  I know 100% in that moment that that man would give his life for me and I would do the same for him.  This is why those men will forever be my brothers.

As we reach the Objective Rally Point I see a few guys in digital cammies.  It was a squad of Marines.  I didn't expect to see that.  We had felt so isolated for what seemed like so long that seeing other US uniforms was almost startling.  When we get to a cluster of trees and see several more men, a feeling of relief comes over me.  Then I see some guy hanging out with his shirt off.  There is a group of Seals sitting around a radio.  In all, a couple dozen Americans from different units were gathered there.  There was such solitude for the last few days I had started to believe that we were the last humans on earth.  It's amazing how isolated those little villages are from the rest of the world, surrounded by hundreds of miles of mountains that make the skyscrapers of our largest cities seem like insignificant toys.

Our first order of business when we reach the ORP is water.  We ask a few of the men pulling security if they have any.  One of the Marines tells us that there are several cases remaining from a resupply drop down in the trees.  What a relief.  We dispatch a fire team to retrieve enough for the platoon. The water had been sitting in the sun for days and was about the same temperature as the water in a tea kettle just before that obnoxious whistle starts.  Just as I am finishing my first bottle my platoon leader calls me over.  One of the guys is down.  Shit!  Now?  Really?

It's one of the squad leaders. As I approach I begin my assessment by simply asking him what is going on. He blinks his eyes a couple of times in an attempt to focus on me the way a boxer does after he has had his bell rung.

"Hey Doc." is all he says.

His breathing is short and shallow. He's lying propped up against a rock. As I begin to remove his boots I tell him to take off his shirt and loosen his belt. His skin is hot and dry to the touch. I'm not at all surprised at this point. I pour some water on his neck in hopes that it would quickly evaporate, helping his body to cool. I pull the blue bag containing the IV setup kit, the very same one that this very same squad leader discarded at our first patrol base. The look in his eyes when I brandish the bag to him was that of embarrassment. He knew that he had fucked up; there was no point in me making a big deal about it. While asking him a series of questions I start the IV on his right arm. By this point this was such a routine procedure that I wasn't even thinking about it, I was on autopilot. While giving my platoon leader a full assessment he interrupted me and gave me the most offhand compliment I think I have ever received. The lieutenant said, "Damn Doc, cool under pressure. So cool maybe you should stick some of those water bottles up your ass to chill them down so we can actually drink them." That would be the only time I ever had a large black man tell me to stick something in my ass and take it as a compliment.

The bird would be here soon. In the swirling dust and debris we board the Chinook helicopter. I can't speak for the rest of the men but that was the toughest helo ride of my Ranger carrier. We were dispatched to find 4 of our brothers, men we didn't know but knew all about. They may have been in a different branch but they joined for the same reasons that we did. They went through the same torture to earn the right to fight alongside the elite. They fought the same fight and bled the same blood. And here we were, departing in their time of need. I know that every other Ranger on that bird would have walked those mountains until their feet were bloody stumps to find those men. We never met them but that doesn't mean that we didn't love them.

When we arrive back at Bagram Air Field we are greeted by our First Sergeant. He shakes each one of our hands and tells us good work. The feelings of ambivalence were overwhelming. We get back just in time for Midrats, which was a meal that the chow hall was open for between dinner and breakfast. Mid rations was mainly for pilots and flight crews that kept odd hours. It was the best meal of the day because you could get breakfast and dinner together. There is something incredibly satisfying about getting waffles with your steak, especially when you haven't eaten more than a couple of MREs total in the last three days.

In the true fashion of the Ranger Regiment we are forced to shave, shower and change into clean uniforms before being allowed to go eat.  We end up missing the chow hall hours because of the order from the senior enlisted NCO and would have to wait until breakfast for a hot meal.  After conducting what would become one of the most significant search and rescue missions in the Global War on Terrorism we wouldn't want to go to get our Fruit Loops and lasagna looking unprofessional now would we?

A man who sat and watched from an office, while sipping coffee, would later reprimand us for not wearing our body armor during the research and rescue.  We were told by that individual that since we were not fit enough to fight in armor that we would have to start doing "combat PT" in addition to our normal workout routine.  This involved going out in the middle of the day, in a full kit, in 100+ degree heat and running for over an hour at a time.  This was put into effect within 24 hours of our return from our extended mission.  Guys were severely dehydrated and likely close to a condition called rhabdomyolysis.  Rhabdomyolysis is a product of severe muscle tissue breakdown that compromises the ability of the kidneys to function.

I still hadn't slept since we returned.  The reality of those A10s dropping bombs so close to us had not left me.  As I lay in my bunk, fighting the pain of exhaustion, one of the privates in my platoon ran into my tent and told me that something was wrong with one of our guys.  There are no duty hours for a medic; your job is those men, always. When I got to him he was seizing on the floor at the gym. His core temperature was well over 100. He should have been resting after that mission but instead he was engaged in a pointless act, handed down by a man who was trying to prove a point. I took Brandon to the aid station where we began active cooling techniques. I delivered my assessment to the doctor on duty. He allowed me to treat the patient myself as he sat back and asked me a few questions. By the time Brandon had a few liters on board, my Platoon Leader and Platoon Sergeant came in. The doctor told them his condition and that I had executed as a medic flawlessly.

This, in addition to my performance on the search and rescue mission that we just concluded, was enough to justify my promotion. My Platoon Sergeant told me that he was promoting me. Nothing feels better than that! I was going to be a Sergeant! My best friends Matt and Jess had already achieved the rank and now I get to join them. I swelled with pride and instantly grew two inches.

"Congrats Doc, you just made Corporal"

What the fuck does that mean? I thought to myself. No one gets a promotion to Corporal. I was already an E4, how are you going to promote me to E4? All of the responsibility of a Sergeant without the respect or pay increase. Thanks again Army, you sure do know your way around a practical joke!

The first sunrise after infill.

Waiting for nightfall to infill to the Kunar province.
These would be our chariots.

This was just before the shots were fired. Notice how steep the terrain is. You can see four Rangers from my platoon if you look closely.

Inside the home of the man that we suspected was the goat herder that compromised the initial mission.

Over watch.

Over watch.  This was just after the baboons rolled up on us.

Close to where we recovered Navy Seal, Matt
Axelson.

Not much would transpire over the next several weeks. We did what Rangers do during slow deployment times. We went to the gym, played video games and got yelled at for lying out and tanning in our short silkies. It was the scene from Black Hawk Down before the mission that we had all grown up imagining. Despite being on the largest US military base in Afghanistan we were completely segregated from the rest of the military. We didn't have to pull gate guard shifts and we didn't have to abide by the rules of the rest of the Army. When we were in the states we never interacted with the rest of the military but to some degree, we had to on this base.

We shared a chow hall and a running track. It was very common to have a First Sergeant or Sergeant Major from another unit stop us because we weren't in the same uniform or our rifle had a bunch of cool guy shit on it that they had never seen. I recall being yelled at while on a 16-mile run for not having a reflective belt on by a guy who I assumed had never actually been on a mission before.

"So the Taliban can't see me!" My response suggested that even with less than two years in, and as merely a corporal, I was already as salty as they come.

Our next big mission of this deployment wouldn't come for several weeks. What started as an action packed trip turned into another long grinding tour, until one night when we were all gathered up right before boarding the helicopters.

"Well, this isn't good," said one of the squad leaders.

"What's going on?" I asked.

"The JSOC Chaplin wants to pray for us before we leave on this mission."

"That's a first! It's probably because we are all going to die" joked one of the older privates.

"Sounds about right," said another.

These guys had an amazing sense of humor. I had been exposed to it as a kid in the fire stations of Peoria, Arizona so it wasn't too shocking. However, these were 19 and 20 year olds that were talking like the firefighters that were friends of my father. Those men had seen 20 years of carnage to become that cynical, these Rangers took the fast track apparently. In just a couple of years of war fighting they had already become as callous as men that had been working civilian EMS for decades.

I image the speech delivered by the Chaplain was a heartfelt one. I, however, was too busy trying to figure out how to work a radio to pay attention. Up until this point I'd somehow managed to avoid having to carry a radio on a mission. To be honest, I don't think that I needed one for this objective either but at this point I was the only NCO in the platoon that didn't have one, a fact that got under the skin of some of the other guys. As a medic I frequently got away with things that other NCO's wouldn't, not intentionally of course. I finally get it to work as we board the Chinook helicopters for what would be my first hostage rescue mission.

Tucked between my body armor and plate carrier is a 3'x5' American flag. I wanted to be able to give a gift to my father upon returning from this deployment that was significant, something to say thank you for all that he had done to support me. I figured that carrying the flag of our country on a historically significant mission would suffice.

We were informed that a _____ contractor had been captured by Taliban forces in the _____ province of Afghanistan. During the Operation Order I ask if our guy has any medical conditions to consider. I am informed that he has asthma so I locate and add an albuterol inhaler to my packing list. I also add a couple of red bulls to my pack. The clock was ticking but as important as speed was to the success of the mission, accuracy would be just as crucial. With these types of missions the stakes are a great deal higher than a direct action kill/capture objective. Our platoon's role was to be infilled a couple of clicks outside of the village to act as an immediate back up plan for the Seals that would be doing a high altitude free-fall parachute jump into the objective.

The flight from BAF was one of the longest I have ever experienced in a helo. We are pulled off target multiple times so as to not compromise the SEALs infill. We hovered around in the back of that cramped Chinook literally all night. We took off at just after sunset and finally got on objective minutes before the sun came up. My entire body cramps up in the heat of the Afghan night. There are guys on top of guys in the back of that floating bus. Despite the uncomfortable conditions no one complains. By the time that we land my legs are cramped beyond belief and I have trouble running off of the back gate into the pitch-black desert night.

We form a semicircle around the back of our rotary winged aircraft to provide rear security for its take off. After hours of incessant noise and vibration it is completely silent, a shift so severe that it sends a shiver up my spine. We sit in place holding security for at least twenty minutes; everyone is on high alert. The sun begins to illuminate the silhouettes of a few of the Rangers to my left and right. It is difficult to tell through the night vision goggles but as soon as things become a little brighter it becomes evident that we are, from a tactical standpoint, in about the worst possible place imaginable. We are sitting completely exposed on a hill with absolutely no cover or concealment. There are ridges to three sides of us that featured large rock formations that would be ideal for enemy sniper positions. Missions like these do not require an officer above the rank of platoon leader; however, it is common for higher-ranking officers to add themselves to the manifest.

They do nothing but get in the way and more often than not they are there for glory, for medals, and as a means by which to potentially achieve their next promotion.  Not all officers are this way but 90% of them are and the one that erroneously put himself on this mission was all that and more. He felt that since he was the highest ranking guy on the ground that he should be calling the shots.  To be honest, he had less than half the combat experience of the youngest private in our platoon and it showed.  His decision was to do nothing.  We sat on that exposed piece of ground for hours in the burning sun with no cover.  At the time, no one knew what was going on.  For at least six hours we sat, waiting for orders and getting burned beyond belief.  Finally the call is made to move us into the rocks for cover.

By this point our platoon was dehydrated and pissed off.  We had been receiving updates that the Taliban had moved the hostage into the hills where we were located.  We had small patrol elements searching but initially came up with nothing.

Eventually _____'s tragic fate was discovered. Someone in the village tipped off the hostage takers about American presence in the village.  We suspected that three Taliban members took their hostage into the hills just outside of the village, his head was with an old band saw.  We call for exfill but are denied.  We are told that it is too dangerous. The 160th has already lost too many birds this rotation and they won't touch down until they can do so under the cover of darkness.  I get a little upset about this.  We have over 30 guys exposed like sitting ducks.  Our lives are trivialized in the grand scope of the fight. It is better to leave us out there than risk losing another helo. I understand the decision but it doesn't make it any less shitty.

By this time the hunger pains start stabbing at me. I could feel my low blood sugar affecting my ability to move. At this point we had been awake for well over 30 hours and we still had at least another six on that rock. Ohhh shit, I forgot about those Red Bulls! The can nearly burns my hand as I pull it from my pack. Down the hatch! I feel my blood sugar instantly rise and I feel alert for the first time since we exited the Chinook. The high would be short lived, however. Within an hour of dusk I crash. I crash hard! I can't focus at all; I'm going to pass out. I didn't really pack any food because this was supposed to be a quick in-and-out. The mission plan called for us to be extracted by dawn. Stupid. In the hundred missions that I would help conduct after this one I never made that same stupid mistake. Food would become as essential on my packing list as ammo regardless of how short the mission was supposed to be. I ask my buddy Nick if he has anything to eat. I feel terrible doing this because I am supposed to be the one looking out for these guys and now I am asking for their help. He produces a Harvest bar from his assault pack and tosses it to me. He might as well have tossed me a Thanksgiving dinner with all the trimmings. It was strawberry and hard as a rock. Most strawberry foods are delicious but strawberry Harvest bars taste like absolute shit under most circumstances, not this time though. I was so grateful for that piece of food. I don't think I would have maintained combat effectiveness without balancing out my blood sugar with that bar. Still to this day I swear that it saved my life.

What could have been another beautiful Afghan sunset is ignored as our platoon positions itself for exfil. I volunteer to carry the man's remains to the bird along with a couple of other guys. The flight crew takes the body bag containing _____ . My Platoon Sergeant and I form a choke point at the tail of the helo to count everyone as they get on. Over the deafening churning of the rotor blades overhead I yell, "WE'RE UP SERGEANT!" I'm the last one to board and try to find a spot in the packed Chinook, there is no place to sit. Except. Except on that body bag. It's a four-hour flight back to Bagram Air Field. I spend the last few hours of that very long day sitting on top of our failed mission.

Our platoon conducted a few other missions on that deployment but the majority of our time was spent training. We had the opportunity to travel to another unit's compound in the mountains. It was a surreal experience having the opportunity to work with them and their facility was absolutely incredible. Tucked into the mountain landscape, the work that they conducted was amazing. They had their own mock villages set up for practicing raids complete with fully furnished houses. We practiced close quarter combat and live tissue training with their unit. I wish that I could talk about it in further detail, however in an effort to respect the secret nature of what they do I must refrain.

We frequently found ourselves at a place called East River Range, which wasn't really much of a shooting range to speak of. It was more like the place out in the desert in Arizona where I would shoot as a kid growing up. Just a dirt road that led to a lot of open desert with a mountain back drop. There was never a shortage of ammo to shoot. Being the medic, I was able to float around and cross train with all of the different weapon systems. The guys from our mortar section were eager to teach me how to lob a 60mm a few hundred meters. The snipers taught with the proficiency of a college professor on windage and trajectory all of their various toys. I was able to throw several rounds through the Barrett 50 Cal. which, needless to say, was cool as fuck! The breachers would show me all the ways that they use to gain access to a building including the shotgun, halligan and C4 charge. We shot anti-tank rockets and deployed claymore mines and threw grenades. As cool as all that was, none of it was as fun as shooting the MK 19 grenade launcher. The MK 19 is a belt fed, air-cooled, fully automatic truck mounted grenade launcher that is capable of hucking up to 60 grenades per minute at a distance of up to 2 kilometers. Typically you fire that piece of war glory in six to nine round bursts, then you wait. The rounds seem to float in the air like a fade away jump shot. Since light travels faster than sound the operator gets to see impact of the half dozen grenades a couple of seconds before hearing their explosion. I can still feel my belly jiggle from laughing like a young child at the joy I exuded from firing that weapon.

We continued to grow as a platoon, teaching one another the skills that we had become specialists in. As I taught the men in my platoon first responder skills they taught me how to do their jobs. We gained a more comprehensive proficiency as a unit. We would need every bit of that proficiency if we were going to survive our next deployment.

Shortly after my 23rd birthday I board the massive cargo plane to return home from Afghanistan for a second time.

Training force on force with simunition rounds on Bagram Airfield.

Shooting mortars on East River Range

Ranger snipers, Steve and Chris reaching out and
touching some targets.

# Chapter 9 - When Skeletons Live

Within hours of stepping off the plane from Afghanistan I'm on my back porch with a beer in my hand. It's early October now and it doesn't feel like a minute has passed since Matt and I were planning our 4th of July BBQ. The two of us sit up most of the night catching up. The sheer gravity of all that has taken place over the last three and a half months is finally able to come out. There is no place for weakness while you are deployed; there is no time for reflection. You have to keep your head in the game. But now that I was at home and had a few drinks, the floodgates opened.

Matt sat with me on the ground in our backyard as I unloaded, brick by brick, everything that I had been carrying from our first mission to our last day in country. I was on the verge of tears when he provided to me a great deal of solace with one simple statement, "You know man, that's just the way it is. Things will never be the same."

I'm not sure why that was so comforting but it was. It made me feel like I wasn't alone in my pain. Matt was always a good friend but never much of a philosopher so his words caught me by surprise a little.

Before going to bed Matt asks me if I want to go to a Notre Dame game the following weekend.

"We can fly into Chicago and catch a ride to South Bend with a friend of mine. My parents have season tickets.  You have a four day weekend next week right?"

"Yeah.  That sounds perfect bud, let's make that happen."  I stay up and finish the case of beer.  When Matt wakes up he realizes that I hadn't gone to sleep at all.  My mind was a tornado, spinning with debris.

"You wanna get breakfast?"  He asks

"Sure," I slur.  It would be the first meal in months that I wouldn't have to carry a weapon to.  As we get into Matt's Jeep his iPod kicks on, *"I'd love to go back to when we played as kids, but things change and that's just the way it is.  That's just the way it is, things will never be the same, that's just the way it is awww yeah"*

"Are you fucking kidding me, Matt?"

"What?"

"Last night when I was dealing with all that shit you quoted me Tupac? What the fuck man?!"  Matt just shrugs his shoulders and backs out of the driveway.  That is the thing about that guy, if anyone else pulled the shit that he did you would hate them for it, but he somehow always managed to come off like such a comedian that you couldn't help but laugh it off.

Driving to IHOP, I can't help but notice how smooth the roads are in this country.  There are no massive holes to avoid from IEDs, the lanes are clearly marked and people pay attention to the traffic signals.  This makes me feel out of place and uncomfortable.  It's difficult to explain but that sense of heightened vigilance becomes a blanket. When the cold harsh winter months turn to summer the habit of that blanket becomes uncomfortable yet for some reason you continue to cloak yourself in it. You don't want to look over your shoulder constantly, it's just become such a necessary habit that it stays with you.

The next few days at work were pretty standard for having just returned from a rotation. We laid out equipment and counted everything. Certain items had to be cleaned and returned. The days were short by Ranger standards. We would have a late work call each day, which meant that we didn't have to be in until 6am and we were released by 1pm. It was common to have a couple of 4 day weekends before having block leave. Block leave is a required two week vacation that the entire Battalion takes simultaneously. For the sake of unit readiness we didn't get to choose when our vacation would be.

I couldn't wait for this weekend. I had never been to a college football game and this was Notre Dame so I knew that we were in for one hell of a good time.

Matt grew up in South Bend, Indiana. He is the oldest of five Irish brothers. When we arrive at his parent's house they welcome me like a sixth son. Matt has an amazing family. I met Matt's father at his Ranger school graduation the previous spring.

His mother emerges from the kitchen as we enter the house, "Hello, you must be Jenkins."

The thought of my friend's mother calling me by my last name doesn't seem at all odd to me at this point.

She gives me a big hug then steps back and looks at me, "I thought you would be bigger."

I'm not sure how to take that exactly. They have prepared a huge BBQ for Matt's homecoming. Matt's friends from college rolled in one by one to welcome him home. I felt like I already knew so many of them from all the stories that Matt had told me. Apparently Matt must have told them stories about me because more than one of them upon meeting me said, "You're Jenkins?! Holy shit! .... I thought you'd be bigger."

We make a serious dent in the beer stash that Matt's parents had in their garage before heading out to the bar. As we walk into the pub, Matt asks if I've ever seen Rudy, without waiting for me to respond he explains that several of the scenes in the movie were shot in this bar. I could give shit, I just want a drink. Matt's parents come out to the bar with us. I'm not sure if it was because they missed him and wanted to spend time with him or if it was because they knew he would do something stupid and despite his position as an Army Ranger they still felt the need to look after him. (Which I completely understand since that guy is always doing something stupid.)

The tray that I carried over to the table was heavy, it should have been, it had eight Irish car bombs on it! It was a good start on the evening as we clink glasses and shout an old toast.  We had a great time reminiscing.  I got to hear all kinds of new stories about Matt.  Apparently he was banned from this very bar years before for attempting to kidnap a midget.  As the story goes, he scooped the little guy up in his overcoat and ran out the door with him.  It actually made a lot of things make sense about the person that I had been living with this entire time.

Up to this point in the evening Matt was behaving himself, which is why it was so odd when he walked back to our table and said, "Well I'm getting kicked out of here in 5, 4, 3, 2 ..."  Before he said one the bouncer grabbed him by the shoulder and said, "Alright smart guy, you're out of here!"

What the fuck, I thought?!  No one at the table has any clue as to what was going on or why Matt was being asked to leave.

I quickly follow them to the front door asking what my friend had done to get tossed out.  The bouncer was clearly a Marine.  I could tell by the tattoos and terrible haircut.  I ask him again.  This time he responds by yelling, "You want me to throw you out too?"

"No asshole, I want to know why you are throwing my friend out?  I'd also like to know why you think you can talk to me that way?"  That got his attention!  By this time we were right outside the front door and I found myself surrounded by four guys.  Two of them were overweight and clearly got the job because they were large, the third guy was a buck fifty soaking wet. The only one I was even mildly concerned with was the tattooed Marine. Our indignant exchange goes on for a couple of minutes before Matt's parents come out to see what was going on.

"Where is Matt?" asked his mother.

Wait a minute, where is Matt? I thought. Did he really just get me mixed up in all of this and wonder off?!

Matt's mother urges me to walk away but I'm in full-blown tough guy mode. I respond to her by saying, "It's alright Mrs. ****, there's only four of them. Easy day!"

In all reality I was about to get my ass kicked but my bluff must have worked because they backed up a little and headed back inside. Just them Matt comes walking up with a sac full of Taco Bell and a gordita in his hand.

"Are you fucking kidding me, Matt!? I'm about to fight four guys for God knows what and you went to get a fucking gordita!"

He just shrugs his shoulders as he turns and walks to his parents blue mini van. On the way back to his house we ask Matt what that was all about. Apparently the bartender was a college nemesis of Matt's so under the portion on his tab that said 'tip' he scribbled in "blow me asshole." A collective sigh and headshake is shared between his parents and I. None of us are remotely surprised by his actions.

Matt and I pass out on the couches in his parent's basement. The next morning I am startled awake by something touching my nose. I grab at it with my left hand and swing with my right! My eyes open mid swing to see that it was Matt's mother playing a joke. I manage to stop the swing just in time. I was still very, very jumpy from my last deployment. The thought of those A10s dropping payload on the Taliban fighters during Operation Redwings floods my mind and I am instantly transported back still clenching her wrist.

As Matt sits up I hear him say, "I told you not to fuck with him while he's sleeping." It takes a few moments for my heart rate to return to under 100 beats per minute.

"Breakfast is ready." She says as she walks up the stairs slightly startled from nearly getting punched in the face.

It was early, but not too early to start our tailgating. A quick breakfast of sausage and beer and we were on our way to see some college football at Notre Dame! It was surprisingly close, maybe a five-minute drive from their home. One of Matt's younger brothers was already there setting up a giant inflatable penguin atop his red Dodge Ram. He had filled the back with sand for a festive beach theme. There were hundreds if not thousands of cars and trucks set up for the tailgate festivities. I had never seen anything like it. College sports wasn't all that important where I grew up so this was all totally foreign to me. People had the most extravagant set ups just to get drunk before a sporting event. There was no way we would find Patrick in this chaos. Then we saw it, the ten-foot tall inflatable Christmas penguin. Okay now it made sense. In all, there were about a dozen of us there, mostly Matt's college buddies. It didn't take long before the large bottle of whiskey started getting passed around. I recall taking a massive pull out of it while standing in the back of Patrick's truck. Mid pull I saw four police officers on horseback stroll up. "HOLY SHIT!!! It's the four horsemen of the Apocalypse!!" I yell in a half-slurred tone. They just signal for me to sit down. I oblige willingly.

We had been in the parking lot for 5 hot dogs, 8 beers and several pulls of whiskey, which if I had been wearing a watch may have been around 2 hours. By this point, many of the people from our group had already entered the stadium. The game was set to start and the horse-mounted cops were trying to get people into the game. As we enter the stadium the sheer magnitude of this place engulfs me. The stadium from the outside is impressive but the history is palpable once you enter the gates. Matt informs me that we will be sitting in the donor section. I wasn't entirely sure what that meant at the time. We walk up a dark corridor to where our seats are.

The experience of seeing the field and tens of thousands of screaming fans was an assault of my senses. It stops me in my tracks. I have never seen anything like this in my life. Matt just slurs, "Pretty fucking cool ain't it?" The usher takes us to our seats. We just keep going and going, step after step, row after row. We are getting closer and closer to the field. We get to the gate directly behind the players on the 35-yard line. We have the first two rows! I look back and see a sea of green and gold, it feels like there are a thousand rows of excited Irish fans behind us. Apparently the donor section was reserved for people that had donated a significant amount of money to the University. There were a couple of famous people sitting in the rows behind ours. One of which was a very popular morning talk show TV personality.

I can't believe where I am right now. Just last week I was sleeping on a cot in a third world country. Again I feel out of place. The sheer number of people makes me feel uncomfortable. A 1st quarter Notre Dame touchdown helps put me at ease. Right before the extra point is kicked I am told that the tradition is to hoist someone up on the groups shoulders and have them do an equal number of push ups as points on the board. I get nominated and willingly accept. This irritates the people behind us that paid a lot for their seats. It irritates them even more when we scored again within a few minutes and I was back up on my friends' shoulders, this time without a shirt on. "Sit down!" the hordes hollered at us. Patrick, who was a student there at the time responded with, "FUCK YOU STAND UP!" Well, that didn't go over so well. I'm not going to say that it was Regis that called security over but I wouldn't put it passed him. We are given our first warning, a warning that we brush off immediately. Every time a good play is made we stand and cheer, an action that does well to piss off the over-privileged, entitled "fans" sitting behind us.

We are playing BYU so needless to say, I'm getting a lot of push ups in. By the third or fourth time that security had to come back to our seats they tell Patrick that he has to come with them. Once again I interject and ask why and once again I get pulled into fray. The security guy, who I am sure was a volunteer, starts to give Patrick and I a speech about integrity and responsibility. I am standing, arms crossed head tilted to the side. Essentially I'm displaying a big fuck you with my body language. After he says some line about how we should learn to grow up I think about everything that I had been through in the last three months and I let out a small laugh. The guy turns his attention from Patrick and looks me up and down. He inquires, "Is there something about this that is funny to you, son?"

"Sir," I reply, "I'm sure that there are plenty of things in this world that I find funny that you don't. This is certainly one of them." Well that pissed him off just right. Fortuitously enough, a police officer was walking by at just that moment. The volunteer hall monitor in the borrowed yellow security shirt informs the officer that we need to go. I just nod my head as I am being flexed cuffed by officer friendly. Hmmm so this is what this feels like. I've snapped flex cuffs on so many terrorist assholes in the past that having them cinched around my wrists was pretty ironic.

As the officer escorts us to the in-stadium holding cell, which was about a three minute walk, we get hooted at by several of the games patrons. Patrick holds his hands in the air and yells, "I guess we love the Irish just a little too much! I guess we cheered just a little too loud!" The people we pass go crazy and cheer for us. I just shake my head and think, please Patrick shut up.

When we arrive at the holding cell the officer asks us what happened. Patrick explains with amazing inaccuracy about a half of what actually took place. At some point he says that I had just returned from Afghanistan a couple of days prior, a fact that the officer takes great interest in. He asks my unit and my rank, my job and my time in service. I am candid and forthright with my answers, a fact I believe he appreciated. He says that he was formerly in the 101st Airborne Division. He administers a Breathalyzer test. Now I hadn't failed a test probably since grade school but this one was sure to mess with my GPA. We started drinking at 7am and it was almost 3 in the afternoon. .07? How the fuck is that possible I thought?! Even the officer is shocked. This goes against what the hall monitor told him, that we were wasted. He begins to believe Patrick's story a little more. Paired with the camaraderie of being paratroopers he decides to let us go.

"So we can go back to our seats then?"

"Hahaha, not a chance," he replied. "You can go home."

"Just so we're clear here officer, right now what you are telling me is that I am not too drunk to drive home, but I am too drunk to go back to the college football game?"

"Yep, but I don't suggest you drive right now."

As Patrick and I have our cuffs removed we are released directly into the parking lot. The first thing that we see is a bar called Legends that shares the parking lot with the stadium.

"Well Patrick, he said not to drive right now. We should probably go in there and sit down for a little while, what do you think?"

"Maybe get a cocktail or two?"

"You read my mind buddy."

Two weeks later we both received certified letters from the University of Notre Dame stating:

*"Dear Mr. Jenkins,*
*Based upon a report by Notre Dame Security*
*Police, I have determined that your presence*
*on the grounds of the University of Notre*
*Dame can no longer be permitted."*

It went on with some other legal jargon but I took it as a big joke. That letter hangs framed above my toilet to this day.

Matt and I at the foot of the giant penguin.

The next six months of training were considerably more exciting than my first cycle. There was a lot of the same stuff that we did before but I was able to get away a few more times on this go around. I talked my way into a couple of schools out of town, one of which being a tactile fighting school called Vanguard. About a dozen of us showed up in Chicago to spend two full weeks learning advanced hand to hand striking, knife fighting and advanced tactical firearms training. It was two of the most valuable weeks of non-medical training that I received as a Ranger. We were put through several scenarios each day that would mimic situations that we were likely to find ourselves in. We were made to walk from one side of a large room to the other, through a crowd of a couple of dozen individuals. Two of them were previously given the direction to attack whenever they wanted. There was no way of knowing who the attacker would be. "Embrace the violence!" was all the instructor shouted as two men pounced strategically from behind. I already had a broken nose and a large gash over my eye from an MMA bout that I competed in the night prior to coming to the course. The super glue that held my eyebrow together was torn apart multiple times during the two weeks.

The course concluded with an opportunity to go head to head with MP5's retrofitted as paintball guns in the shoot house of one of our government agencies. I'm pretty sure that I learned more about close quarter combat on that one day than I had over two deployments.

Other training trips on this cycle included a trip to Tacoma, Washington to cross train with some Air Force Pararescuemen and Seal Corpsmen. Also in attendance were a few corpsmen from the regular Navy. Training with other special operations medics from various units was not abnormal but I hadn't really had much interaction with conventional forces since going through RIP a few years earlier. I had grown to expect a certain level of experience and knowledge from guys that we went to schools with. It was really interesting seeing how they responded to the amount of and advanced nature of the information provided at the course.

By civilian standards, the procedures taught at this course were incredibly progressive. In addition to the shock lab that I described earlier we did nerve blocks on one another, learned advanced surgical techniques for field operations and started intraosseous infusion on each other. Getting a fast one is like getting punched in the chest with half a dozen needles, actually getting a fast one IS getting punched in the chest with a half dozen needles. The primary needle punctures the sternum so that fluid can be absorbed directly into the bone. This is necessary if a patient has lost so much blood that getting an IV started on the vein is not possible. The two-week course concluded with another live tissue lab that was significantly more comprehensive than the one that we did at SOMC.

A couple of months later I would have the distinct privilege of attending my second hospital rotation, this time in Atlanta at Grady. There were only two of us this time and we were only the second group to come through. As a result most of the hospital staff didn't really know how to treat us. Most of them treated us like paramedics and had no clue the level that we had been trained. Being a special operations medic is very much a double-edged sword. Through the course of your training and experience you become one of the most capable, well rounded medical personnel in the world yet no one outside of your tiny community really has a clue as to what you are capable of. As a result you are treated like an EMT basic and told to hold the patient's head when they come in with multi-systems trauma.

There are exceptions to this, however. Our preceptor for this rotation was a brilliant surgeon named Doctor Jeff Salomon. He gave us reign to do whatever procedures we felt comfortable doing. I had the opportunity to treat more gun shot wounds during those three weeks than I had in the collective previous three years I had been in the Army. Those 14-hour days at Grady Hospital would prove to be priceless for what was about to come.

It was early 2006, I had just been promoted to Sergeant and my platoon had earned the top spot as the primary battalion effort after a top performance at platoon evaluations. Platoon evals was a three day training event that tested every aspect of a platoons combat effectiveness and capability. With the exception of a couple of brand new privates that just joined our platoon, our entire element had several combat deployments. We had refined our ability to communicate with one another and had become a very well oiled machine. We would need every bit of that proficiency as we stepped of the back of that cargo plane for the third time. This time we would be stepping off into Tikrit, Iraq at a time that was approaching the most violent in the history of the war.

At the FBI shoot house during Vanguard.

Vanguard training is as real as it gets.  My boy Josh "embracing the violence"

Tactical knife fighting at Vanguard.

......

## Chapter 10 - Grave makers and Gunslingers

"Hey Doc, wake up!"

I wasn't... I didn't even finish saying, I wasn't sleeping. The door slammed shut and Josh had moved on to wake up the next chu - an 8x8 cell like, connex box that we lived in while working in Tikrit, Iraq in the summer of 2006. NCO's and officers got their own rooms, privates typically had to double up. Even with two overgrown Ranger privates in an 8x8 room it was still hands down the best living conditions that I had experienced on any of my deployments.

This must be important, Josh usually talks shit for at least a couple of minutes. I glance over at the clock, its 16:00 so most of our guys were just waking up. I poked my head out of the door to see a handful of guys headed to the makeshift plywood Joint Operations Center (JOC).

"What's up?"

"Come on Doc, let's go. Mission brief in 5."

As usual I had no clue of what was going on. Even now as a Sergeant, somehow I still seem to evade the chain of information passed through the platoon. I decide that shower shoes aren't the best footwear choice for this occasion and quickly get dressed. I walk in just in time to not get more than a dirty look from my platoon sergeant. I half heartedly listen while a certain officer that most everyone in our company had a great disdain for babbled on about two guys in a safe house that we would be our primary kill/capture objectives. We would fast rope in utilizing UH60 "black hawk" helicopters. He said some other things but honestly I was hungry and this was about as routine a wake up call as the alarm clock that awakens most college students. We had only been on this deployment for a month and had already executed dozens of successful direct action missions.

Wheels up at 19:00. So by the time that medal hungry Major finished his bloviating, we would have a little under two hours to eat and get our mission essentials together. For me that meant making sure that I had plenty of snacks in what I referred to as my "moral pouch." I'm telling you right now a watermelon jolly rancher is better than Christmas morning to a six year old when you've been on an objective for two days! I will also tell you that half of being a good medic is about keeping up the moral of your guys. When we were on the QRF for operation Redwings I handed out a lot more candy than trauma medicine.

The boys from the 160th Special Operations Aviation Regiment (SOAR) pick us up right on time, which as usual was just past sun down. Those guys are about as nocturnal as they come and more than once I was grateful for their outstanding ability to operate under the dark of night. The feeling of letting your feet dangle out of the door of a Black Hawk helicopter a couple of hundred feet off the deck is unmatched. On this day, however, I was pushed to the back jump seat, which meant that I would be one of the last guys on the ground.

The flight is short and the hot night air feels good as it swirls around the inside of the bird. When we arrive Josh quickly gets his fire team to the front door as the Black Hawk pulls away showering us all with BB sized pebbles and debris from the open field that we had recently landed in.

We are less than 100 meters to the target house as we begin to advance. Second squad was approaching from the side of the building. Weapons squad was set in a blocking position behind the target house in the event that anyone attempted to run. As we moved closer to the tiny house in the middle of that field, it happened.

I feel the heat from the blast from 40 meters away, everything is white, sound is reduced to a high pitch buzzing and then, silence. There is nothing. Time stops. I wait to hear someone scream out for the medic. I wait for something, anything. Every ounce of air has been drawn from me as I wait, a lifetime in that single breath, I wait. As my eyes regained focus I realize that the blast came from the exact position that second squad was just in. The predator drone feed would later show the blast's heat pattern completely white out the screen and erase the six Rangers that stood within a couple of meters of the suicide bomber's position.

Air rapidly enters my lungs the way it does after you've been held under water a little too long. I look immediately to my platoon Sergeant and we run. Not to cover, not to safety but directly at that shack of a house, in the middle of that field, in the middle of nowhere. Josh's fire team reaches the front door just in time to receive a volley of 7.62 slung at them from a PRK set up on the other side of the shacks mud wall.

They do not hesitate. They act. They run into the throat of that monster, directly through the door that has the business end of a very large automatic weapon pointed at it, at the helm of that weapon is a man hell bent on their demise. They do not hesitate. They act. At this moment I notice someone running from the objective directly toward weapon squads position. The only thought in my mind was watching second squad disappear at the hand of a suicide bomber just seconds earlier.

I raise my rifle. It's dark and he's 75 meters away but the green beam illuminating from my PEC2, only visible by night vision goggles, locks on his chest. Go on and pull that trigger. Squeeze. Squeeze. I didn't even realize it but I instinctively come to a complete stop to take those two shots. As the figure dropped I continue to run. I'm not entirely sure why but I change directions. Instead of running toward the front door, I begin to run to the motionless body that just a breath ago was standing. I'm within 15 meters. BOOM! I feel it. A second blast. This one was much closer. My exposed face is peppered by what feels like tiny ball bearings. I stay on my feet; my eyes never lose focus of the white tunic laying 45 feet in front of me. I will later learn that this blast came from a frag grenade thrown by my good friend Allen in an effort to clear the back room of the shack. The sound of controlled pairs being squeezed off hasn't stopped by the time I reach him. For the second time in the longest minute of my life my breath is stolen from me. He's a boy and he's still breathing.

I am going to be completely honest. I don't remember the next few minutes. The world kept moving and I am assuming that I did too because the next thing I know I am kneeling over one of the members of second squad talking with another medic, John. He was okay. This guy just had a suicide vest detonate within spitting distance, how the hell is he alive? As I look up I see Thomas, second squad leader. He is directing the rest of his guys. They are alive. They are all alive! How? I am at a total loss for words in this moment. I am not a pious man but in this moment I would bet you a hand full of Chili's coupons that those men were recipients of a little divine intervention.

I begin to tend to some of their minor wounds as I realize that first squad took heavy fire upon entering the building. I hand over care to John and quickly make my way to the front door. The mangled flatbed truck where the suicide bomber sat up and proclaimed "allahu akbar" is etched in my mind. I see what looks like his legs

and most of his body. His head is completely gone. My best guess is the vest was poorly constructed and the brunt of the blast traveled up rather than out. His head is found, in tact, 30 meters away; popped off like a cork on a cheap bottle of Champagne. He should have paid more attention in shit head school. I reach the front door. The small room had already been cleared and the guys from first squad are in search mode by the time I enter. I ask if everyone is okay. All I get is a couple of uneasy laughs.
Apparently one of the 7.62 rounds grazed one of the younger guy's helmets.

The room is small and filled with smoke from the gunfight. There is a hole just big enough for a man to crawl through in the back corner of the room. Apparently several men crawled through the hole to another room as first squad made entry to the first room. After eliminating the threat on the PRK, Allen tossed that frag grenade into the back room rather than chase the men on his hands and knees. I joke with him that nearly blowing me up in the process will cost him a beer when we get stateside, he just shrugs his shoulders as if to say welcome to the "I just got blown up club."

There are a couple of lifeless bodies on the floor in the front room. One was slumped over the machine gun; the other must have drawn the short straw. He got to be the last guy to get to crawl through the room's only egress. Just as my desire to poke them with a stick draws me one step into the room I hear my call signal called on the radio. It's my platoon sergeant. Second squad is chasing someone that our eye in the sky spotted fleeing the target house. I immediately run to their location. By the time I get there the company commander is giving an order to a good friend of mine named, Nick.

Nick and I had recently been promoted to Sergeant at the same time. Now Nick has always been a very good Ranger. In addition to saving my life with that disgusting strawberry Harvest bar in Afghanistan he was smart, well spoken and well liked among the guys. Several factors that influenced him being promoted so quickly. Nick was also very good at taking orders, normally.

They had one of the men pinned down in a sort of a reservoir. The Company commander wanted Nick to send one of the guys on his team down into the reservoir to grab the guy and try to pull him up the side of the reservoir that was about eight feet high.

In the kind of tone you would expect a Ranger Sergeant to address a superior officer, Nick asked, "Sir, you want me to send one of my guys that just got blown up by a suicide bomber into that hole and grab another potential suicide bomber, throw him on his shoulder and carry him up that eight foot mud wall?"

"Roger," replied the Captain.

That's not exactly what happened. Nick responds in a way that I will never forget and in a way that I will not repeat here.

Just about the time that incident is resolved another call comes over the radio requesting my presence on the north side of the target house. As I approach I see Eric, Nathan and our interpreter standing over the boy who I shot earlier. He is still breathing, in fact he is talking. As I kneel down to assess his wounds I ask the interpreter what he is saying. I notice that he has more than just two holes in him. He was hit from multiple shooters. For some reason I now feel less responsible for his situation. The interpreter says that the kid is 14 and came to Iraq from Saudi Arabia. I asked him what he is doing in Iraq. As long as I live I will never forget his response.

"I have come here to kill Americans!"

"Then why did you run?"

"There are too many."

"How did you get here?"

"They paid me to come."

"What would your parents think if they knew that you were here?"

"They would be proud."

Without hesitation I turn and walk away. I have the power to help and do nothing. To this day I have yet to fully process this decision. Guilt? Shame? Ambivalence? I don't know how to feel about it. I am not sure what emotion to affix to such an event. I know that he lived because of the efforts of one of our other medics but I did nothing - a fact that keeps me up some nights still.

As I walk back to the target house I see the severed head of the suicide bomber, fully in tact. It doesn't even faze me, I just walk by it. Once back in the house I link up with my friends from first squad. They have just finished searching the house for any possible links to other cells in the area. The place is an absolute mess. I notice something that I can't help but laugh about. At the feet of one of the dead terrorist lay a couple of bottles of a *7UP* knock off drink called *CHEER UP*. I pick it up and Matt takes a quick picture. Someone cracks a joke, "Feeling down about getting blown the fuck up? Have a refreshing glass of *CHEER UP*!"

Josh takes a bottle back home to the states and uses it's contents to make mix drinks in his barrack room. Those drinks were amazing too. Tasted like liberty!

Just as we are calling for exfil a call comes over the radio. We are getting an add-on mission. Abu Musab al-Zarqawi has just been seen less than a hundred miles away. For those who are unaware, at the time Zarqawi was the Iraqi equivalent of Osama Bin Laden; he was high value target number one. We make our way back to the exfil point and wait for the Black Hawks to return. As we wait, a thermo baric bomb is dropped on the house, which on that night served as a crucible for 1st platoon, erasing it from existence but never from our memory.

Not a word is spoken on the short helicopter ride to Balad. Call it exhaustion, or quiet reflection on what just occurred but no one uttered a word. Each member of the platoon stepped off the bird and onto the tarmac at least 2 inches taller than they had when they had woken up that morning. We walked through the doors of the hanger in the middle of the night as if we were one single organism.

There was a contingent of Rangers that had just watched our entire mission from the drone feed. We were caked in dirt and blood and possessed a certain saltiness that we didn't previously carry. As the adrenaline slowly wore off I looked to my left and right and saw a certain grit in even the newest private in our platoon's eyes. One of those men was a Ranger named Nicholas Irving. Irving would go on to be one of the most deadly snipers in Ranger history and write a book on his accounts as a Ranger sniper. Knowing that this would be my final deployment as a Ranger it felt like a sort of passing of the torch. The things that these young Rangers would learn on their first deployment would serve them well in the years to come.

There were at least a dozen old green cots set up in that hangar where men sat as they reloaded the black 30 round magazines that had just been emptied. Batteries were replaced in NVGs and camelbacks were topped off. As exhausted as we all were at this point, we knew the night was just getting started. I am amazed as I check over the members of Second squad that had just had the closest encounter with a suicide bomber possible. A few minor burns and scratches but nothing beyond that.

As I finish treating some of the men with some simple dressings my Platoon Sergeant calls me into a small room in the back of the hanger. He hands me a box filled with atropine auto injector. (The AtroPen® Auto-Injector is indicated for the treatment of poisoning by nerve agents.) He asks me if I can give the platoon a short refresher on the use of the AtroPen and tells me that Zarqawi is believed to be held up in a chemical warehouse and is likely to use chemical weapons on our platoon as we enter.

It probably came off as a pretty smartass comment but I had to ask, "Sergeant, you want me to go out there and tell that group of guys that there is a chance that after all they have just been through that they may need to stab themself in the leg to keep from having their insides melt?"

He understood that I was being sincere, that I didn't want to see those men be put in harms way again but we both knew that that was our job. He didn't say a word, he didn't have to. I walked out and started handing out the little handheld injectors as though they were pieces of Halloween candy. I get a few confused looks, a lot of shoulder drops and headshakes and one big fat grin. He knew that I wasn't handing these fuckers out as a joke and I think that he truly reveled in the idea of getting his hands a little dirtier.

The men stand with professionalism as I give the quick tutorial on how to self-administer the drug into the outside part of the thigh. At the end of the instruction I ask if anyone has any questions, only one man speaks up.

"So Doc, our faces might get melted off tonight?"

"It's a possibility," I respond.

"Cool."

We once again climb aboard the Black Hawk helicopters en route to uncertainty. As we take flight we are informed that the mission is being called off. Some of the men are disappointed, the ones with families are relieved and the rest are indifferent. We all know the acts that this man has committed warrant his absolute demise and would love the opportunity to be the hand of vengeance. None in the group would hesitate to do so but at the same time none of these men carry a death wish. Be smart in the way that you hunt and you will live to hunt another day, become overzealous and you get replaced by a folded flag handed to your next of kin. Ironically enough this would not be the platoons last shot at Zarqawi but for now it was time to call it a night.

Inside the foreign fighter safe house. Snagged myself a war trophy that would later be used to mix drinks with back home, "Cheer up."

......

## Chapter 11 - There Will be Justice in Murder

Each 24-hour period begins to look exactly like the one before it. Wake up at three in the afternoon, go to the gym, check on any missions that could be developing, eat "dinner" and wait.

By sundown we would be checking the batteries in our radios and ensuring that we have all the necessary supplies to get through another night raid. An hour or so after the sun sets we get picked up by a group of Black Hawks and are delivered to the doorstep of another Jihadist.

One of these hundred nights seems to stand out from the rest, however. We get Intel on an individual that our big brothers have been tracking for some time. He is a tier 1 target and has been evading capture for some time. The appropriate plans are made and once again we find ourselves with feet dangling from the open door, the hot summer desert air stinging our faces.

A split second before the bird touches down I hop from my position in the door of the Black Hawk. My feet welcome the embrace of the uneven soft dirt field. I know that Allen and Josh will be racing me for this one. Getting to be the guy to pull the trigger on this particular shit head will be huge bragging rights. The people inside already know that we are here. There is no way for them not to. Four UH60 Black Hawks just landed in their front yard. Tonight speed is security. The faster we can get to the front door, the less time our enemy will have to prepare for the inevitable assault. Not that there is much you can do to prepare when thirty Rangers are running at your front door in the middle of the night. I get to the door a split second ahead of Allen, Josh and SFC Bent. Somehow I end up as the third man in the stack.

We don't sit on the door, we flow instantly. We have rehearsed this hundreds if not thousands of times. Allen breaks left and controls the first corner; Josh enters the room and heads right. I follow Allen to the left and SFC Bent follows Josh to the right. Allen and I have a door directly in front of us. Without so much as a blink of hesitation we enter the interior door. A figure in the far corner is holding an AK47 oriented on the door that we just entered with every intention on spraying us with 7.62mm rounds. As if it occurs in slow motion his rifle jams giving Allen the opportunity to acquire his target. The man fluidly transitions from his AK47 to a frag grenade. As his finger embraces the pin he receives two perfectly placed rounds to the face, carrying the contents of his skull out the back of his head. He drops atop the grenade and we brace for impact. It doesn't explode. This mule's seen his end in love and war.

We hear two more shots from outside of the room. Someone just engaged a target running toward the room that we were in. Flash bangs are going off all over the place. This is the definition of controlled chaos.

Shots are ringing out from outside the target house and I can't help but think that this must be what war feels like.

The following excerpt is the account of the Ranger sniper team on the roof that was with us that night...

Flying into the target area, we could see the house. We came in low and fast as we landed on the X. When we flared and came in to land near the red/black corner, I put my laser with the flood on to help illuminate the darker areas and windows of the building in hopes of putting down potential threats to the UH-60 Blackhawks we rode in. We landed a mere 50 meters from the house to serve as the containment and isolation element. There's an unspoken competitiveness among us Rangers concerning where you sit in the bird. We don't really talk too much about it, but the ones who have enough rides in a 60 know their chances of getting a kill drastically increase when you sit in the door. They're even better when your door is facing the target building. The isolation element was a two helo package. We had two sniper teams on this mission, my partner Myles was with me, and Isaiah and Jake were on the other Isolation helicopter. The pilots were precise and efficient with our infill. Before the dust settled and the beat of the helo's rotors were gone we heard shots fired inside of the house. We hadn't even had a chance to get in position and the fight had already begun. As the first shots rang out, I witnessed a shadowy figure clumsily leap out of a window on the red side of the target and begin to trot in our direction. In true Ranger fashion, I witnessed ten lasers converge on this man. He obviously had no idea we were out there because he was running directly at us while toting an AK by the receiver with one hand. Out of fear and

cowardice, he took the path of least resistance and fled the
ensuing controlled, chaotic, and methodical violence that was
overwhelming his fellow terrorists inside the house. Either way
he was met with a wall of lead and his body function was turned
off like a light switch. The other bird landed slightly closer than
ours and I had the pleasure of watching my best friend Isaiah,
sprint up to the mangled body of this squirter and put two more
M118LR in him, just to make sure he wouldn't have any life left
to squeeze the trigger. Myles ran right beside me as we headed
for the house to gain access to the roof. I remember jumping
over his lifeless body as we headed for the roof and getting a
good long look at him. He was tall and fat. A terrified look of fear
was permanently frozen on his face. It was him. Hamadi Tahki. I
recognized him from the pictures in our pre-mission brief.

As quickly as it began it was over.  One man
lay dead in the kitchen and another in the room
that Allen and I entered just moments before.  We
begin searching the men, both living and dead.  I
kneel down over the man's body and find another
weapon system.  It was a police issue Glock 19.  We
had been finding these on objectives with greater
frequency these days.  The pistol was covered in
human brains and little pieces of the man's skull
that Allen had just moments prior fragmented.  I
put the pistol in a Ziploc bag and placed it in my
pocket. The spoon was still in the grenade so we
carefully replaced the pin and added it to a pile of
weapons that were collected throughout the house.
Only once before have I seen a human head
look this way.  There was no actual structure to the

man's skull.  The face was still in tact for the most part but it more closely resembled a flaccid mask than a human head. When I was 19 and working as a firefighter in central Arizona I was dispatched to a call where a gentlemen had been struck by a large pickup truck while walking down the freeway at night.  It was the first time I ever saw a body mangled to such an extent and it stuck with me. Here in this tiny dust filled bedroom in Iraq I am transported back to that cold, rainy highway outside of Mayer, Arizona.  It is a sight that I am much more capable of coping with this time around, however.

The evening becomes quite routine at this point.  We go through the home looking for any material that can potentially lead us to the next objective.  We question some of the young men and women that were in the house, take pictures and package what we think can be valuable.  By this point I was thinking that if we hurry up we could get back to post in time for midrats.  I know I've mentioned midnight rations before but honestly it really is the best meal of the day.  You can get spaghetti and cereal in the same sitting, waffles and steak with a side of eggs and mashed potatoes. Glorious.  Years later an ad genius at Taco Bell coined it "Fourth Meal." He must have been a Ranger!

It was common for there to be a shit hole outside of these little mud houses and this one was no exception.  As we began to make our short foot movement to our exfil point where the Black Hawks are set to pick us up we notice a large hole in the ground several feet deep filled with human excrement.  Now if you've never walked around in the dark on uneven terrain wearing night vision goggles (NVGs) it isn't easy.  The one's that we were using at the time did not provide depth perception so rolling your ankle in a hole was somewhat common.  The headquarters element including the company commander and my good friend Nathan were the last to make the movement to the exfil point.  By the time that they were leaving the house our chalk had already set a perimeter around where the helos would be picking us up.  I could see the writing on the wall as the Company commander walked out of the target house.

He was easy to identify due to the two large antennas towering over his shoulders from the multiple radios that he carried.  I watched in anticipation as he approached that deep hole full of human shit.  Elbowing my Ranger buddy to my right and pointing toward the house, he looked just in time to see the Captain disappear into the cavernous shit abyss.  There was a collective attempt at controlling laughter from the entire squad as it would appear that we were not the only two privileged enough to see the boss take the plunge.  With all the strut that a Ranger Sergeant possesses, my buddy Nathan calmly side steps the pit fall and continues to the extraction point.  The joke would eventually be on us, however, as rather than throwing away the soiled uniform the CO decided to wash it communally with the rest of the platoon.  For weeks our entire element smelled like human waste.  Still owe you one for that move, sir.

By the time that we get back and download all of what we seized and conduct our after action review, the sun is cresting over the desert landscape and the chow hall is just opening for breakfast. A half dozen of us decide to forego showering immediately for the lure of a hot meal. Outside of the chow hall on most forward operating bases are giant barrels, half buried in the sand with a baseball sized hole cut in the top of them.  They are referred to as clearing barrels and are intended to be used to safely unload your weapon before entering the chow hall.  The thing is, most people on a forward operating base never actually have a round in the chamber because they act in a support capacity and seldom, if ever, leave the front gate.

Being a medic I carry an M9 pistol as well as an M4 assault rifle.  This is in the event that I have to engage an enemy target while simultaneously working on a wounded individual.  It is also highly convenient when traveling around base because it means I don't have to carry that bulky ass rifle.

I feel a tap on my shoulder as I go to take my first bite of runny scrambled eggs.  It was a Sergeant from another unit that I did not recognize. He said to me in a nervous voice, "Sergeant, your weapon is condition orange." Now I have no fucking clue what that means.  All I know is that I am hungry.  I know that we just got done laying hate on a bunch of shit head terrorists. I am covered in dirt and I still have the remains of that man's brains on my right sleeve. So I replied the only way I knew how. "Cool bro." I then turned to take a bite of my breakfast and received a second tap on the shoulder. The man persisted,

"You have a magazine in your weapon, Sergeant."

"You're Goddamn right I do, homeboy. This is Iraq, not Disneyland."

"You can't have a mag in your weapon in the chow hall, Sergeant."

I'm not proud of it but I lost my cool at this point. I'm not sure if the compounding stress had got to me or I was just that hungry. I did not maintain my professionalism. I stood up and looked that man of equal rank in the eyes, drew my side arm from the holster, dropped the mag on the table and cleared the round from the chamber. His eyes got fucking huge. The man was just doing his job but at the time I didn't care. He had just woke up from a full nights sleep in a comfortable bed. I feel my right eye tick a little. It's the first time that I can recall this happening. It still does it to this day in certain situations when I become irritated or feel threatened. I ask him if he wouldn't mind leaving me the fuck alone so I can eat my fucking breakfast. He didn't know what to do. He started to say something about the clearing barrels outside being the proper something or other. I simply sat down and continued eating. I imagine that he just turned and walked away.  One of the young privates just said, "Jesus Doc!" and continued with his soggy waffle.

......

## Chapter 12 - Delirium Trigger

After several weeks the days and nights begin to blur together. I'm not sure what day of the week it is anymore. This is, hands down, the most pain I have ever been in. I haven't slept in over a week at this point and I think I can officially self diagnose that I have insomnia. We've been on mission every night for as many nights as I can remember. Everyone in the entire platoon has been fed a constant stream of adrenaline since we landed in Mesopotamia and I think it's catching up to several of us at this point. I've handed out my entire supply of Ambien to the guys that I feel need it more than I do so I lay in my bunk staring at the ceiling. It's Iraq in the summer and since we work at night, our down time is midday, and it's fucking hot here! Growing up in Phoenix was hot but Iraq in the summer is fucking hot! As my eyes close and I attempt to find my first moments of sleep there is a tap on my door.

"Hey Doc, sorry to wake you but the compound is flooded."

"What?"

"Yeah, ummm I think the Euphrates overflowed or some shit."

Of course it did. This deployment hasn't been eventful enough we should add a flood, maybe a plague too. Our compound was tucked right between where the Euphrates and the Tigris met.

It was surrounded by 20-foot tall concrete barriers that apparently were not set with any sort of foundation.  When the water pushed under them it eroded the parched dirt beneath causing them to topple over.  As if having helicopters crash, people blow themselves up and getting shot at wasn't enough now the walls of our own fortress were trying to kill us!  These things had to weigh at least a few tons and were toppling over like dominoes all around us.  Command made the decision to move our entire platoon to some tents that were on the other side of the forward operating base.

Now I'm not the type that needs any serious degree of luxury, hell I've passed out on the floor of a Motel 6 in at least a dozen different states but these new living conditions fucking sucked!  They each had about a dozen old cots in them and had apparently been standing in the desert heat since the initial invasion three years prior.  The constant exposure had left them literally see through.  It was 120 outside the tents and 130 degrees inside.  This should definitely help the guys get some much-needed sleep!  At this point we all just laugh.

"Fuck it!  We're all gonna die out here anyway, we can sleep then," jokes one of the team leaders.

The jokes would be short-lived. Our platoon Sergeant pokes his head in our shitty excuse for living quarters and tells us that we just pulled a mission.

I am borderline delirious during the mission brief.  It feels like Groundhog Day and these Red

Bull knock offs have no more effect than a little can of water.  I can only imagine what drinking 10 of these "Rip It's" a day has done to my kidneys.  Nephron, cortex, loop of Henle.  FOCUS!  You're in a mission brief for fuck's sake!

Okay I'm on chalk 2, we are assaulting a target house containing known bomb makers.  We go through the motions of jocking up as the sun falls over the desert.  Our flying chariots touch down in an empty field a few hundred meters from our shitty tent village and we disappear into the night once again.

I don't even remember the flight or the infill.  The first shots that rang out on the objective startled me awake.  Ah, there is my nightly adrenaline fix!  I've got my feet under me know and me and my boys from second squad are chasing a couple of guys through a fig orchard.  The UH6 "little bird" helicopters are circling above giving us a play by play on the direction that the two squirters were headed.  They started doing gun runs on those poor bastards.  There really isn't much that you can do when those guns open up, the 160th pilots are the most accurate in the world.  They are the reason why a lot of special operations guys that I know are still on this earth.

For all you would be terrorists out there, just a heads up, hiding in the dark is easier when you're not wearing a body length white tunic.  We spot one guy laying on the ground to our right.  Nick's fire team goes straight for him, pouncing like a pride of lions on a fucking zebra. Joe and I advance past toward the second target. His hands are up and both of our rifle barrels are locked on his center mass. We are both at a full sprint at this point, moving toward him with the knowledge that the violence of action is the only thing that can keep us alive. I knew that Joe had him covered. In a full sprint, I dropped my rifle down to my side by way of the sling and struck that man with such force that he literally went feet over head nearly completing a full back flip. The best part was thanks to the technique that I had recently learned at that tactical fighting school in Chicago it didn't hurt my hand one bit. Thanks again Vanguard!

Joe covers me while I zip tie the man. Meanwhile one of Nick's guys who was securing the first squirter tells him, "Sergeant, my hands are all wet." We avoided using white lights on missions because they have a tendency to make a quick target out of the person holding it. A quick check would reveal that the gun runs being made by the little bird pilots were effective. The man had a softball size exit wound on his inner left thigh. That gaping hole made it tough for him to walk all the way back to the initial target house but that was his fucking problem. None of our guys were going to carry him. Not after the reports came in from the other squads that were clearing the house letting us know that the house that they had just fled from was full of bomb making materials and pictures of high value U.S. targets. No, this shit head gets to walk. You may think that is inhumane but then again, you've probably never been blown up by a suicide bomber or watched as a group of your friends are erased by one.

When we got into the house I was able to see the extent of his injuries. That man's scrotum was torn open and his left testicle had completely unraveled as a result of that helicopter raining down hate from the sky. All I could think at that moment was, holy shit that was a good shot! The man was screaming in agony by this point as I stood over him. Empathy? What the fuck is that? I had none at this point. I was perfectly content to watch that man roll around in agony until we ex-filled. He had a tourniquet on to stop any major hemorrhage but I hadn't made any effort to pack the wound or help with pain management.

The company commander must have heard the screams from the other room. He came in and asked what the situation was. He was former Special Forces so he frequently considered the "hearts and minds" as being an important part of every mission. I'm not going to get into the dynamic of how each faction of special operations works but I will say that the Green Berets in special forces typically have a slightly lighter touch than their Ranger counterparts. He told me to administer morphine to the man and pack his wounds. Now this man outranked me by a lot but not when it comes to patient treatment. On the ground the medic is the authority on all things medical. He was right though, I couldn't just leave the guys nut dangling out and someone might trip over it. I calmly explained to the CO that I don't carry enough morphine for him and you both so maybe I should hold on to the narcotics that I have in case one of our guys get laced open tonight.

As I knelt down over the man I wasn't quite sure how to treat an uncoiled testicle. For all of the crazy scenarios that were drilled into us in SOMC, oddly enough, this one never came up. I decided that I would use it to help pack the wound in his leg. I can't imagine how that must have felt packing that thing into his open wound with Kerlix then wrapping it with a trauma dressing without any morphine. A testicle when uncoiled is actually quite long. It took almost a minute to pack the entire thing into his open wound.

Just as I was finishing up I was told that there was three more squirters in the orchard that we needed to secure. We formed a small element to track them down. With the air assets that we had circling overhead we figured that it would be a quick game of hide and seek but in reality it took most of the night. We trudged through uneven muddy fields for hours taking direction from the guys overhead until we were exhausted. One by one we found all three men and they were not happy when we did, mainly because we weren't happy that we had gone on a three hour death march to locate them.

I'm not going to sugar coat it, I punched one of them in the dick. Hard. Then placed my thumb in the wound that was created by one of our service dogs and used it like a joystick while we looked for his other two buddies. This isn't something that I'm proud of but it isn't something that I'm ashamed of either. It is simply the way that war is, it's how it makes you and if you haven't been there then you can keep your humanitarian opinion to your damn self. By the time we got back to the cluster of target houses we realized that we weren't the only one's putting in a nights work.

Apparently a pretty significant firefight went down in one of the houses. One of the snipers engaged an enemy target through the window of the house. It was an absolutely amazing shot. He was on the rooftop across the street and saw the figure running toward the front door that one of our fire teams was about to make entry on holding a rifle. One shot, straight through the neck. When I examined the person I could tell pretty quickly that, one, it was a woman and two, she was pregnant. When I informed the sniper that made the kill shot of this detail it didn't seem to affect him in the slightest. In fact, he grinned the same grin that he did in that hangar in Balad when I handed him that atropine injector.

We piled up all of the bomb making materials and weapons and disposed of them with an incendiary grenade outside in the courtyard. We had a haul of prisoners and information that would likely lead us to the next mission, the next target house filled with people that want us to die.  Nearly every night for over three straight months we punched the time card and went to work.

After the mandatory After Action Review (AAR) we headed back to our tents.  It was 10am by this point and the desert sun was just starting to seep through the transparent tent ceiling.  There isn't even a point to lying down.  I escape to the gym in an attempt to burn through this adrenaline.  My tiny silk shorts and plain brown t-shirt would make me stick out like a sore thumb in the regular Army gym filled with squads of vibrant, well rested military personnel in their grey Army PT uniforms, complete with reflective belt and bad haircut.  I get even more dirty looks as I am the sole gym occupant doing Olympic lifts and muscle ups in the corner in an attempt to cope with all that had transpired.  It would be another full week and a half dozen more missions before I slept.

One of the final missions that I went on as a Ranger was in June of 2006.  Like so many of the nights before we were tasked with finding, and if need be, eliminating a high value target.  We landed in a small valley about a kilometer from the target house.  It would be a straight sprint up.  About half way up I felt an aggressive pop in my abdomen.  My right leg felt very heavy all of a sudden.  I would find out later that my abdominal wall had ruptured.  Slowing down wasn't an option.  We made it to the front door of the target house and cleared it with the precision of an experienced surgeon. We didn't even have to talk to each other by this point in the deployment as we moved seamlessly through this dark house. We clear every single room and find ourselves on the rooftop where about a dozen women and children had been sleeping. This was somewhat common in Iraq in the summer months as it was typically cooler on the roof than inside the house.

The ground floor had been secured and it appeared as we had just hit another dry hole. As was the common practice after the all clear had been given, we began conducting a search for sensitive materials and weapons. I was in a room by myself looking through a series of dresser drawers. I found a significant amount of material on bomb making as well as documents that would connect the homeowner with Saddam Hussein. When all of the drawers had been tossed, I focused my attention on a basket of clothes near the window. I knelt down to sift through the soiled white tunics. Just as I did my left ear picked up an odd sound, it was a type of buzzing that I was familiar with but had not heard in awhile. I looked left but it was too late, the buzzing was gone. So naturally I went back to sifting. No more than ten seconds later I heard the noise again. This time, I immediately look left and see a glow just above my head. FUCK! That's a cell phone! That is a cell phone in a terrorist's pocket! That is a cell phone in a terrorist's pocket in a hidden location less than a foot away from me!  I am on my feet in a fraction of a second, weapon orientated on target, safety off, finger on the trigger!  But I don't squeeze.

Now the story originally went, he lunged at me and I fired.  Not so much.
I actually called for the guy in the other room, we will call him Steve for the sake of the story.  Steve was in the room in an instant.  I very briefly told him what happened and both of our M4 carbine assault rifles were fixated on the corner.  We couldn't see the man because he was hidden very well behind a closet door.  That's when it happened. Steve said, "Doc, we should shoot this guy."  As soon as he uttered those six words the door moved violently, startling me. I let a volley of eight shots loose on his position.

Immediately after that man's body hit my feet, a call came over the radio to determine where the shots came from.  I lost my composure a little. My superior officer asked who fired the shots and all I could say was, "Umm, It was me."

Now that seems like a reasonable answer except that there were about 40 of us all connected on that channel.  If you knew this guy, you would know that his response was something close to, 'yeah, and who are you asshole?'

Then I broke another cardinal rule by saying my name rather than my call sign. (For those who don't know, a call sign is simply a number or nickname assigned to help soldiers maintain anonymity.)  I gave my location and within seconds a good friend of mine entered the room and gave the lifeless man two more shots to the head for the sake of being fastidious.

One of my superiors gave me a high five, and like that it was over. I told my story, or at least the slightly modified version of it that I believed wouldn't get me brought up on charges to my bosses boss and then his boss. They were all giddy. I didn't understand. Later I found out that the man that I shot was one of the primary high value targets in all of Iraq. He was a "bad guy," a really bad guy, by our definition. So why should I feel bad, I eliminated a total villain.

Here is the crux. I received a medal announcing to the world that I am a hero for eliminating a threat to our nation. In reality, I become a murderer while giving this man martyrdom. Or did I have it right the first time? I guess if you ask my family they would say that I am the hero, if you ask his family they would say that he is. But then again my family has never heard the real story, but his probably hasn't either. They likely didn't know that he was responsible for the death of hundreds of people. That he had used that very cell phone to detonate roadside bombs. Does it matter? I don't have the answer to that. All I know is that as I sit here typing, that God forsaken award hangs from the wall over my right shoulder. And if I did not covet honor so much I would burn it like the piece of hypocritical trash that it is.

Returning from another all night mission.

Flying over the Euphrates. Summer of 2006.

Nothing feels like this. My good friend Josh and my feet dangling from the door of a Black Hawk helicopter a hundred feet off the ground.

Josh and Christian on the front stoop at the beginning of the "Great flood of '06

.......

# Chapter 13 - The Broken

A couple of days later I was sent back to the states to have the tear in my abdomen surgically repaired. My platoon would stay in harms way for three more weeks. They have even more stories about the hit on Abu Musab al-Zarqawi and a little bird crash that I missed out on. Missing out on that action really sucked but not being there for my guys was terrible. I barely slept for the next three weeks waiting for them to return. I drank literally everyday and not in a celebratory fashion. Knowing that my brothers were still in harms way was unlike anything that I had ever experienced. I was glad to be home but hated myself for telling anyone about my injury.

When my platoon returned we celebrated in true Ranger fashion. One of my mentors was getting out of the army right after they got home. I've never been very good with goodbyes but by this point in my military career I had become no stranger to them. Dave was a little different though. We had worked together as platoon medics for a few years now. Dave taught me a lot of the little things that make a great medic. He had been a role model for me when I first got to battalion and his leaving was like having a big brother move away from home. I believed that this separation would be easier if everyone was already a little drunk by the time that I arrived so I hung out at home until I had received at least a dozen, "where the fuck are you, doc?" voice mails.

A "little drunk" doesn't even begin to describe the condition that Dave was in by the time that I arrived.

There are a handful of guys from our company that I recognize as I enter the bar. Dave is slouched over at his bar stool with his forehead resting on his left forearm.

"What's up buddy!?"

Dave pulls his head up and attempts to focus on me. It is apparent that lifting his head at this moment caused him more trouble than the last time I watched him start an IV on himself in the dark. His head bobbles around for a bit before falling back on his forearm, which was lying on the bar. I look back at my good friend Nathan, "He's not looking so good."

"Oh Dave's fucked up!" Nathan says with a laugh.

Nathan was the Charlie Company Commo Chief by this point, which meant that he was in charge of all radio communications for the company. Nathan is a burly Viking of a man. He has hands like hammers and stands over 6 feet tall.

I start to ask Nathan how long they've been here when I hear the violent splatter of Dave throwing up all over the floor.

"Ahhh shit, Dave just puked. We're totally getting kicked out of here." Nathan says while laughing. Dave wipes the vomit from his mouth with his sleeve while picking his head up to see if anyone noticed. He plays it off with a move that I certainly did not expect. He gets the attention of the bartender and orders another shot! The stones on this kid! There is no way in hell that that bartender is going to ... and he is pouring Dave another shot!! What the fuck!? He shoots that Jager like it's a 5-meter target. Just as I start to say, what a champ, Dave puts his head in his other arm and throws up down his other pant leg.

"Maybe we should go," Nathan says

"Yeah, that's probably not a bad idea," I respond.

We paid Dave's bar tab and help him out the door. Most of the other guys had relocated to a bar across the street so it was just Nathan, Dave, Flippy and myself. Flippy was our company's training room NCO. He was a good guy, not very imposing but well liked among the guys. Needless to say, Dave isn't walking very straight. There was a lot of construction going on in downtown Columbus at the time so there was an 8' tall chain link fence that ran the length of the curb creating a sort of corridor. The sidewalk was about 10 feet wide and we had a row of bars and shops with to our left and that chain link fence to our right. Nathan and I were walking behind Dave, laughing as he repeatedly stumbles into the huge windows of the store fronts.

"Hey! Asshole knock it off!" Shouts some random guy standing outside of Scruffy Murphy's. So of course Dave now intentionally slams himself into the next large window. Well this pissed that guy off. He started speed walking toward Dave. I know that in his condition there is no way that Dave will be able to defend himself. As the guy gets within a few feet of my Ranger buddy I hockey check him into the wall. I think this caught him off guard, he may not have realized that we were friends with the guy he was trying to pick a fight with. In true douche bag fashion he puts his hands up completely exposing himself and exclaims, "Bitch, you don't know me!"

I respond, "Well, you don't know me," as I punched him right square in the mouth. Now I have competed in combat sports for years. I have a winning MMA record and I have attended several special operations tactical fighting schools. I've received and delivered more punches that I can possibly count but I am telling you right now that I have never, never hit someone so square with such force. That guy's knees buckled and he went down like a limp sack of shit!

As he hit the ground I hear a ringing similar to what I experienced when Allen's grenade detonated a little too close to me in Iraq as I get punched right in the ear. What the fuck! Where did that come from? As I turn and face whoever it was that struck me someone else pulls my shirt up over my head hockey style. Where the fuck did that come from? Now I'm getting punched from two different people and I can't even see who they are. I am swinging wildly to try to create some distance.

I manage to get my shirt off completely. A quick assessment of the situation reveals that Flippy is flat on his back getting his face stomped by a couple of guys. It looks like we kicked a hornet's nest. There are eight of them. Where the fuck did they all come from? I look to my left just in time to see Nathan one punch some guy in the face. As the guy is falling down Nathan turns and services another target, and another. I am in absolute awe. He just knocked out three guys in a matter of seconds. I look to my right and what do I see? Yep, Dave has a hold of that chain link fence. He is kneeing the shit out of it Muay Thai style screaming, "Fuck you bitch!" Dave just started this whole thing and his drunken ass is fighting the chain link fence. Classic.

I knock one of the guys stomping on Flippy's face to the ground. This gives Flip enough space to get up. I start backing up preparing for one of these idiots to pull out a weapon. As I am backing up I bump into someone. I turn to face him, fists up, ready to strike. To my surprise the guy is in uniform. He has on a beautiful tan beret. "You Rangers?" he asks.

"Roger" I reply.

"I'm staff duty, come on let's get the fuck out of here."

Nathan and Flip grab Dave and we back away. The three guys left on their feet are trying to help their five buddies up and don't attempt to chase us. The staff duty truck was across the street. Just as we were getting in we see those damn red and blue lights. SHIT! As the cop steps out of his squad car I see two girls walking down the street. I change direction and begin walking with them acting like I don't know those other guys. It almost worked too. Almost. The officer hollers at me and I respond that I don't know those guys. Like most things I attempt to turn it into a big joke. He collects all of our IDs. Well Shit! Looks like we're going to jail. Just as he has all of our licenses, some absolutely random guy in a muscle car pulls up and yells, "FUCK YOU" to the cop and peels out. The officer hands our IDs the staff duty NCO and tells us to wait here as he gets into his car to chase that beautiful drunk asshole that just burnt rubber.

"So you guys want to wait around for that cop to come back and arrest us?"

"Fuck that!"

"Yeah, good call Nathan!"

The staff duty NCO takes us all home, one by one.

The next morning when we arrive at Battalion, Flip has a boot print tattooed on his face. Dave and Nathan are hung-over beyond belief. I still can't believe Dave took that shot of Jager after throwing up. After our morning formation, Nathan decides that he is going to go home. This wasn't the first time that he decided to cut out of work 11 hours early. We created an award called "Soft Skill of the Month" that Nathan had won for the last five months; this would ensure that his streak would not go unbroken.  A "soft skill" is a term used to describe anyone who has a job other than infantry. Having a job like medic, comms, training room, or cook would qualify you for our made up award. Nathan had won in previous months for taking a long nap in the cab of a truck during squad evals while everyone else was training in the rain.  He said that he was monitoring the radio and there was no point in him getting wet if he didn't have to. Another month he had me remove a tumor from his left arm to get out of doing a jump.  The standing rule is that you are not allowed to jump if you have stitches.

So Nathan wasn't around when we got called into the First Sergeant's office.  1SG Sealy was nicknamed "The Rhino" and for good reason.  The man's legs were thicker than my waste.  He was built like an NFL linebacker with close to twenty years as a Ranger.  He was the only First Sergeants I had ever known to have a beer with the privates in his company.  He knew that the strength of the Regiment was the men and he was always willing to listen to their opinions about things.  On this day, however, he arrived to work and received a phone call from staff duty informing him that some of the guys in his company were in a drunken brawl the night before.  That put him in a bad mood.

I was running sick call in my aid station when Flip came in and told us that the 1SG was pissed and we had thirty seconds to get into his office. The ass chewing that followed could be heard by the guys in the chow hall.  He.  Was.  Pissed.  I remember him saying, "When staff duty told me that some of my Rangers got in a fight downtown while we were on IRC, I thought I was going to have to kick four privates out of Ranger Battalion.  Then I find out it is my senior company medic, training room NCO and commo chief.  Wait, where the fuck is Nathan?  You assholes know that if you had been arrested you would have fucked the entire company?  What the fuck were you thinking you dumb ...."

I interrupt him, "1SG..."

I realize that the question that he was asking was strictly rhetorical and he didn't really want any of us to say a damn thing.  His eyes get even bigger as he focuses them directly at my soul.

"...1SG, we were only doing what we were trained to do, we were looking after another Ranger."

He takes a deep breath in.  He wants to destroy me right now but I can see in his eyes that he knows that I am right.  "GET THE FUCK OUT!!" He yells.

We don't hesitate.  The three of us scurry for the door the way a dog does when it's been kicked in the ass for shitting on the rug.  We get back to the aid station and call Nathan, he doesn't answer.  He's probably sleeping.  What a shit head.  At least he doesn't have to walk around the rest of the day with a boot print on his face.

....

Just a few weeks later it would be my turn to say goodbye to this chapter in my life. Like my first return from overseas there was no ceremony. Everyone was busy preparing for another training event. There was no going away party when my time came. My platoon sergeant, a man who I have a world of respect for joked that I was always getting over when there was work to do. I told him that it had been an honor being his medic and shook his hand. I walked back into my aid station for the last time to hang my dog tags from the ceiling along side each of the medics that had left before me and walked out the door without anyone noticing.

....

## An End Note

I had visited 46 states and drank a beer in every one of them. I conducted hundreds of real world missions as a special operations medic, some good, some bad but everyone a learning experience. I helped some men to live while taking the lives of others. I was trusted with the health and well being of our nations heroes. I learned more about myself in a couple of years than most men will in a lifetime. I lost friends and gained tattoos and scars. The confidence that I would take away from this experience is, to this day, my most valuable character trait; it is also what alienates me from most people. Most importantly I worked side by side with the best men of our generation. Men that would have no doubt fought beside Leonidas at Thermopylae had they been born 2,500 years sooner. These men are the greatest hope of our generation. They are altruism, they are benevolence. They are terror in the hearts of the enemy. They are blue collar farmers and college graduates, doctors and business owners. They are fathers, brothers, and sons. They have carried the burden of our nation. They are my friends, my brothers, and forever will be.

## More cool guy pictures:

The high-speed life of a Ranger medic! This was inside the aid station where Dave, Dano, Smith, Matt N., Lewis, John G. and the other medics of Charlie Company spent most of our time.

Flying someplace cool to do something badass in Afghanistan.

Me, Jess, and Matt Ranger school graduation.

Some of the medics from C-Co 3/75 a couple of
weeks before I got out in October 2006.

Waiting for ammo to show up at a range in Ft. Benning.  The younger enlisted went head to head in wacky bat races to entertain the NCO's.  20 spins then a 40-meter sprint to the closest tree.

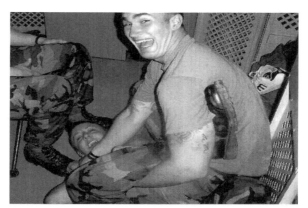

This is why our AO was referred to as "The Zoo," constant shenanigans.  It wasn't uncommon for a full on no holds barred fight to break out.

Fast rope training in Bagram, 2005.

Oh, it's your birthday?  Salerno, Afghanistan.
Winter 2004.

The lighter side of war. Afghanistan. Winter of 2004.

Nicky P. and I being ninjas during training on
Ft. Benning, Georgia.

I would like to give a special thanks to everyone that helped out during the writing/editing process...

~Marty and Blackside Concepts for providing direction and allowing me an outlet for my drunk rambling on *Hit the Woodline.*

~Jack Murphy and the guys at SOFREP publishing a couple of my stories, ultimately giving me the courage to write this book.

~Lindsay for editing this thing in what must have been world record time.

~Brian for providing several pictures, including the cover

~Nasty Nate for sending that zip drive with all the pictures and videos of our time in Iraq that helped my memory.

~Michael, Jack, Christina, Mark, Nick, Gwen, Jess and everyone else that read the very rough draft and gave me feedback.

~Alexander for providing the accounts of our encounter with Hamadi Tahki.

~ Jameson Irish whiskey for providing the liquid courage to tell stories that I've spent the better part of a decade trying to forget.

~My dad, Bruce. For teaching me that it's "cheshire cat" ....among other things.

16160936R00108

Made in the USA
San Bernardino, CA
20 October 2014